HOMING

AMERICAN LIVES

Series editor: Tobias Wolff

HOMING

INSTINCTS OF A RUSTBELT FEMINIST

Sherrie Flick

UNIVERSITY OF NEBRASKA PRESS | LINCOLN

Acknowledgments for the use of copyrighted
material appear on page 163, which constitutes
an extension of the copyright page.

The University of Nebraska Press is part of a land-
grant institution with campuses and programs
on the past, present, and future homelands of
the Pawnee, Ponca, Otoe-Missouria, Omaha,
Dakota, Lakota, Kaw, Cheyenne, and Arapaho
Peoples, as well as those of the relocated
Ho-Chunk, Sac and Fox, and Iowa Peoples.

♾

Library of Congress
Cataloging-in-Publication Data
Names: Flick, Sherrie, author.
Title: Homing: instincts of a rustbelt
feminist / Sherrie Flick.
Description: Lincoln: University of Nebraska
Press, 2024. | Series: American lives
Identifiers: LCCN 2023053645
ISBN 9781496238542 (paperback)
ISBN 9781496240637 (epub)
ISBN 9781496240644 (pdf)
Subjects: LCSH: Flick, Sherrie. | Flick, Sherrie—
Family. | Authors—United States—Biography. |
Women authors—United States—Biography. |
Feminists—United States—Biography. | BISAC:
BIOGRAPHY & AUTOBIOGRAPHY / Personal
Memoirs | LCGFT: Essays. | Autobiographies.
Classification: LCC PS3606.
L533 Z46 2024 | DDC 813/.6
[B]—dc23/eng/20240227
LC record available at
https://lccn.loc.gov/2023053645

Set and designed in Fournier by N. Putens.

CONTENTS

ACKNOWLEDGMENTS

Enormous thanks to the many people who helped *Homing* become a reality. From conversations to book-and-article recommendations to interviews to writing and editing help to moral support to long walks and many cocktails at Kelly's and Dish, the village kept me at it. Mainly, this book wouldn't exist without Hattie Fletcher. Her encouragement, editing insights, and friendship were my lifeline into nonfiction. Next in line is Danielle Chiotti who pep-talked me over a dinner at Dish into *trying*. Sarah Shotland's consistent attendance at Booth cannot be understated. My editor Courtney Ochsner, Mary Brice, Kati Csoman, Ladette Randolph, Alice Julier, Beth Kracklauer, Elvira Eichleay, Christine Stroud, Brittany Hailer, and Joy Katz— key. Big thanks to my copyeditor, Hope Houtwed, and my project editor, Kayla Moslander.

I began drafting this essay collection and revised it for years at the essentially important and creatively uplifting annual Quaker Lake writing retreat with Milena Nigam, Hallie Pritts, Sharla Yates, Lisa Robinson, Bergita Bugarija, and Stephania Vega. I also had the gift of two writing-time getaways at Marilyn Meyers' magical cottage on the Chesapeake Bay, for which I am so grateful. A Writing Pittsburgh Fellowship from the Creative Nonfiction Foundation initiated this entire project along with support from In Fact Books. Thanks for believing in me.

I have so many incredibly helpful mentors, friends, editors, and family members: the Flicks (especially Don and Shirley), Hilda Raz, Sandy Yannone, Liz Ahl, Chauna Craig, Elizabeth Kadetsky, Ryan Schnurr, Brian Butko, Melissa McCart, Stacey Harwood, Peggy Wolff, Doug Heuck, Linn and Marilyn Meyers, Guy Capecelatro III, Pam Raiford, Nancy Krygowski, Steve Pesci, Christopher Fortier, the Scoobs, the Scrappy Motherfuckers, Ceres Bakery (especially, Penny Brewster, Lyn Voss, Jennifer Richmond, Gail Brewster, Kris Lanzer, Maura Driscoll, and Cheryl Krisko), Charlyn Ellis, my Holt Street neighbors (especially Roberta Stoughton), Diane Cecily, James Simon, John Fleenor, Yona Harvey, Tara Rockacy, Chris Ivey, and Bubby & Jo-Jo (who are dogs).

Extra thanks to all the people who took the time to sit down and talk or email with me for these essays: Penny Brewster, Mary Brice, Amy Camp, Margaret Cox, Kati Csoman, Michael Elmer, Anthony Fillipelli, Dan Flick, Don Flick, Jeff Flick, Stephanie Flom, Brittany Hailer, Beth Kracklauer, Michael Moore, Peter Oresick, Charles Rosenblum, Rick Schweikert, Eugene Shephard, Christine Stroud, Lyn Voss, and Ed Waldo.

As always, so grateful for the love and support pouring in from my guy, Rick Schweikert.

HOMING

LABORING THROUGH

Jonathan Neumann and I board the campus shuttle, which carries us about twelve miles southeast toward the coast from Durham, New Hampshire, to Portsmouth, New Hampshire. It's November 1985, a crisp winter day. We've bundled into our mittens and scarves and now wander the crooked streets of this formerly raucous port town. Jonathan hails from Durham, North Carolina, and this is his first real winter. He's ecstatic about the snow. You can see the exclamation points emanating from his body.

In high school he played drums for the Slushpuppies alongside Mac McCaughan, who in 1989 would go on to cofound the '90s legendary indie rock band Superchunk. Jonathan and I meet in Honors Anthropology 101. He has a giant brown-haired afro and wears old-man button-up thrift-store shirts and lots of bead necklaces and bracelets. I wear a pink backpack and light blue Keds. He makes mixtapes for me that include Billy Bragg, Robyn Hitchcock, the Meat Puppets, and Hüsker Dü. Bands I have, of course, never heard of. I write an essay about culture that our professor reads aloud to the class because he loves the sheer beauty of the language, and maybe this is the first moment in college when I feel like a real writer.

Durham, New Hampshire, where the school is based, is a predictably quaint one-way-main-street New England university town that even has a little stream running through campus. Portsmouth emanates a different vibe. Settled along the Piscataqua River, with Kittery's active shipyard just across the way, there's sun and water—and activity. Tiny stores with sweet plate-glassed displays line the cobbled streets. People mill around in Market Square, shopping, and chatting at coffee shops and cafes. All this vibrant, civic, forward movement is otherworldly to me after growing up in a dead Western Pennsylvania mill town surrounded by decidedly unquaint, dying businesses. In my memory a thin layer of dust covers everything in downtown Beaver Falls. We shop at the Beaver Valley Mall. We eat at Eat'n Park restaurant. I have not been trained to participate in this kind of bustling, arty small-town life. It seems so easy and happy and bright. I will fit in, though. I feel myself breathing, smiling. I don't know it yet, but these are my people.

Paul Revere rode through Portsmouth to warn that the British were coming. Vestiges of its port life still remain. Lobstermen unload at the docks. Seedy biker bars and tiny tattoo shops pop up along the street face. But there's also an alternative community of artisans, a funky alt-newspaper *Re:Ports*, bakeries, bookstores, a mug and candle shop, and a soup restaurant.

Working artists rent studios right along the water in Portsmouth. Café Brioche, where I will soon procure a summer job, sells traditionally made croissants, baguettes, and batards across town from Café Petronella, which cooks up American fusion cuisine—curried vegetables and bitter greens salads. There's the Button Factory, an artists' collective and Generic Theater, which pulls together plays here and there, recruiting students, lobstermen, and school teachers as actors. The early '80s had seen an artists' renaissance in town, and those artists took the tired port city up a notch. Soon Portsmouth discovered the commodity of *tourism*, and in years to come it will wring the last drop of it out of these streets.

Back then, we ventured into Portsmouth when we could. There was live music at the Press Room and a little holistic herb shop, the Mustard Seed, on State Street. After I move there I attend free theater and music in historic Prescott Park each summer. Josie F. and Mary E. Prescott worked as public school teachers and in 1940 used their inheritance to buy up dilapidated industrial riverfront property along the Piscataqua to create the 10-acre park.

This idea of preservation stands in stark contrast to where I'm from, where aging mills stand idle and abandoned, recent history in plain sight. Where the city of Pittsburgh uses riverfront property to build a jail. By remembering the town's history, Portsmouth itself seems able to forge ahead into reinvention by telling its own story to the public. There are historic home tours and Strawbery Banke, an outdoor living history museum. In 1985 no one is interested in the history of the steel industry. It's still a dirty secret, where I grew up. In my freshman composition class I write an essay quoting a series of unemployed steelworkers interviewed by my hometown newspaper the *Beaver County Times*. My professor says, "I know places like this exist, but I never hear about them." It seems like time travel, moving from Western Pennsylvania to New England. I'm moving from the past to the future. A geographic magic trick.

I head home in 1986, the summer after my freshman year, returning to Beaver Falls, Pennsylvania, a mill town still in the throes of high unemployment and economic depression. All my high school friends are home too. Only a few of us find jobs. Men who once labored in the mills now work at the local McDonald's and Burger King. The passenger train that had run daily from Pittsburgh to Beaver Falls stops that year and never starts back up again.

But, ironically, the macho image boasted by the steel town remains in place. "As a powerful steel center the Pittsburgh region has long been known as a sooty, hard-working, blue-collar, beer-drinking city," writes Maurine Greenwald in her essay "Women and Class in

3

Pittsburgh, 1850–1920" in *City at the Point*. "In stories, songs, and paintings, Pittsburgh figures as a 'man's town' characterized by labor's muscle and brawn amidst industrial smokestacks, brilliant furnace fires, corner taverns, and rough-and-tumble sports." It doesn't matter that those smokestacks now run cold—no fires burning through the night, no grunt and pull.

Bars fill with the simmering unemployed. Removing the day-to-day industrial labor does not take away the long-entrenched, male-centered bravado of the place. Just as having multiple losing seasons doesn't take away the hero status of the local football and basketball players. If anything, it makes them dig in even more. In Lois Weis's 1985 ethnographic study *Working Class Without Work: High School Students in a De-industrializing Economy*, she affirms just this. The loss of labor jobs in an industrial economy pushes the white high school boys to double down on their domination of both women and people of color. Without easy access to a macho, physical laborer identity, they demand it even more. The jocks rule the school. Intellectualism is for sissies. The sexist, racist patriarchy is alive and well. A haze of desperate depression hangs over the tree-filled hills and valleys, a trusty river snaking through.

No musician and album better represents the working-class machismo of the region better than Bruce Springsteen's *Born in the U.S.A.*, which is released during my senior year of high school. We attend Springsteen's Three Rivers Stadium concert for that album's tour in September 1984. My high school friend Eugene Shephard camps out at the Beaver Valley Mall to score us tickets. He remembers buying the sleeveless white T-shirt with the album cover on the front—Springsteen's super fit butt in faded Levi's with a red handkerchief in his pocket, the American flag his backdrop.

Springsteen is a tiny speck down on the stage in Pittsburgh that night. The sound is ridiculously horrible. But still, I want to be the girl he pulls up on stage during "Dancing in the Dark," just like he does with short-haired, fresh-faced, Ked-wearing Courteney Cox in the video playing on everyone's MTV.

"The President was mentioning my name the other day, and I kinda got to wondering what his favorite album musta been," Springsteen says that night. "I don't think it was the *Nebraska* album. I don't think he's been listening to this one." Then he plays "Johnny 99," about a laid-off worker who can't find a job and gets drunk and shoots a clerk during a messed-up robbery.

The next night he dedicates "The River" to Steelworkers Local 1397 and encourages people to give to the food bank. The first established in the United States, it was organized by unemployed women steelworkers.

I don't follow politics enough to understand why he plays "Johnny 99" that night. But now I understand that President Ronald Reagan had gone off-script in a speech in Hammonton, New Jersey, two days earlier on September 19 and tried to own The Boss after Springsteen had already politely declined endorsement. And, as we all know: nobody owns The Boss.

"America's future rests in a thousand dreams inside your hearts. It rests in the message of hope in songs of a man so many young Americans admire—New Jersey's own, Bruce Springsteen," Reagan crooned to the assembled crowd.

Reagan, running for his second term against Mondale—who scored the Crosby, Stills, and Nash song "Teach Your Parents" for a controversial ad that interspersed young children's faces with ballistic missile rocket launches—got the idea about Springsteen as an emblem for his "Leadership That's Working" campaign from conservative George Will. After attending a Springsteen concert wearing a bowtie and double-breasted suit jacket, Will wrote a *Washington Post* op-ed, which conveniently misidentifies the song "Born in the U.S.A" as a pro-American, pro-Republican anthem professing easy, white-washed rah-rah patriotism. He seems to have blanked on the lyrics that aren't the chorus of that song, with their in-the-trenches subtext, cynicism, and irony, which analyze an America failing so many. But Republicans will employ this little trick for decades to come: co-opt that which isn't theirs by simplifying and stripping away complex meaning.

"Springsteen's tour is hard, honest work and evidence of the astonishing vitality of America's regions and generations," Will writes. "There still is nothing quite like being born in the U.S.A."

What I remember that night at the concert while dancing in my seat amongst the jean jackets, T-shirts, mullet haircuts, and sneakers is everyone singing every single word of every song.

Adoration for The Boss in Western Pennsylvania cannot be overstated. He represented us up there on stage, an us winning at life. But part of being us had to do with the subtext of missing out, out of labor, of the tradition of muscle and grit that we had lived and that still lived within us every day. The Boss plugged his amp directly into that.

Working-class youths in the 1970s and '80s were cheated out of an identity, Barbara Johnstone argues in *Speaking Pittsburghese*. "Rock stars like Bruce Springsteen, Billy Joel, and John Mellencamp sang about alienated working-class kids, and movies like *Saturday Night Fever* (1977) and *Hoosiers* (1986) depicted their struggles to overcome what was suddenly the adversity of being working class." The buff and newly muscled-up, bandana-wearing 1984 Springsteen pounding away on his guitar in his jeans and T-shirt manifested a solution. "The many and complex labor questions of the 1970s seemed to have found easy answers in the 1980s with the narrowing and hardening of white working-class identity into a blind national pride that sounded like belligerence," writes Jefferson Cowie in *Stayin' Alive: The 1970s and the Last Days of the Working Class*. The tricky sleight-of-hand that happened next made the emblazoned white working-class male the emblem of *both* the down-and-out working class and the rising Young

Republicans. Redneck had a convenient appeal across the board for white men of the time.

This is how many true-blue union Democrats suddenly found themselves voting for Reagan, and it's how two groups with not much in common know all the words to the same songs.

What becomes clear in the summer of 1986 is that the post-industrial mill town world doesn't have much to offer me. I can maybe be the girl pulled up on stage to dance like Courteney Cox in Springsteen's video, sure, but I can never be the powerful musician banging away on his guitar. And it occurs to me that I actually want to be the guy playing guitar. I want to be that guy. Powerful. In charge. Writing things other people consume.

The summer I travel home to Beaver Falls after my freshman year of college is the last full summer I spend in Beaver Falls, the last time I live more than a week in my parents' house. I return to school in New Hampshire, to my English literature degree and my minor in philosophy, to creative writing classes, to handknit sweaters and pottery mugs, to musicians and artists and people discussing books at café tables, the sun pouring in, the ocean nearby, gulls circling overhead.

I move to Portsmouth in 1987 and room with Scott Houston, a musician, artist, and baker. I date a philosopher. I date a poet. I'm at home and out of place. I live in a kind of homeland where I don't totally know the local language. I have a hard edge I can't smooth down. It sticks up like a cowlick if something seems too pretentious, or it pushes me to the corner when I don't understand these new customs of ease and communication. I want in, but I'm out. But I want in.

One day I stumble upon a little homestyle place on Penhallow Street called Ceres Bakery. It's warm and inviting, with whole wheat baguettes, linzer tarts, coconut cream cakes, shortbread cookies, and homemade soups and quiches for lunch. The Mexican tile tables and the baked goods jumbled inside the antique display case draw me in.

Acoustic music plays via cassette tape over a battered stereo speaker. A big bank of windows along the storefront lets in the natural light. Friendly workers scurry about in the open kitchen and behind the counter, bantering with each other and the customers. I apply for a job by writing out why I want to work there on a brown paper bag. Owner Penny Brewster still takes applications this way thirty years later.

I'm hired as a counterperson and then soon I'm working from 1:00 a.m. to 4:00 a.m. as an apprentice baker with head baker, metalhead, and water-chugging hellraiser Shelley Cole, who quickly puts me through my bread-mixing, rising, rolling, and baking paces. Shelley exudes a simmering repression and no-bullshit anger I immediately relate to. It's like a homecoming of sorts, and I come out the other side, most but not all mornings, highly caffeinated and still able to lift my arms without pain.

In a few months I graduate to my own midnight to 7:00 a.m. bread-baking shift, where I reject Shelley's heavy metal and instead blast the Velvet Underground, Blondie, and the Pixies. I frequently head straight to class from work, sharing baked goods with my professors and fellow students, flour smeared over my T-shirt and jeans. I'm proud to be a baker. I feel powerful alone in the bakery at night. I love my work. And maybe it's this connection to labor, the physical power of my body, that lets me into this new, alien world while remaining loosely tethered to the old one. My astrological sign is Cancer, so scurrying in sideways always makes sense.

Back then the bakery's fifteen employees are all women, and, with the exception of one, they're all seven to seventeen years older than me. I'm twenty-one. Clear skinned, clear eyed. Ready. Here's my chance to have the older sisters I've always wanted.

These women have liberal arts degrees and work as artists, artisans, metalsmiths, and seamstresses while they also work at the bakery. They fix their own cars, sail their own sailboats, grow their own food, knit, quilt, drink, smoke, and swear like sailors.

It's here that I zero in on my brand of feminism. Not based in ideas floating in classroom theory (although formed by those ideas) but instead practiced on a daily basis and manifested in how women run their businesses, how they interact with vendors, how they talk to customers, how they talk to each other, what they wear, what they think about relationships with men and women, and how they help each other out.

Penny Brewster is twenty-eight years old in 1980 when she opens a bakery on Ceres Street, a few blocks over from Penhallow. She buys two buildings on Penhallow Street three years later, and that's where Ceres Bakery moves to and still thrives now—a squat little building once painted pink but is now light blue. The bank questions more than once why her husband isn't signing the mortgage papers along with her, and vendors often ask for the manager when Penny steps forward to sign for an order. "When I started, there were maybe two other women-owned businesses in town," Penny tells me on a nice, sunny July day in 2015.

A metalsmithed, apron-wearing, long-haired goddess with a wand rises above the outdoor wooden sign. There are flowerboxes over the windows and chairs lining the front of the building along the sidewalk. There's a line out the door. Penny has just recently, reluctantly started accepting credit cards. She still doesn't have Wi-Fi, and no plugs are available for computer charging. At home I have photographs of me and my friends posing in front of the bakery in men's blazers and thrift-store dresses, in shorts and tank tops, with homemade haircuts that evolve into salon cuts, gray hair, and Dansko clogs that span every decade since the '80s.

No one baking there has formal training. It's homestyle at its best, with recipes coming from grandmas and cookbooks and a great spirit of experimentation and how-to in the place itself. "It was very organic from the start," Penny says. "We sort of meandered in order to find what worked and what didn't."

These days Penny has long white-gray hair that she winds up into a top bun while she's working. She still makes a lot of her own clothes—loose dresses and pants in vibrant purples and blues. She has a mischievous smile that often does not belie what she schemes to do.

Penny attended my same alma mater, the University of New Hampshire, in the 1970s and became interested in what it would mean to take the women's rights movement off the streets and into a business. "I was a giant feminist in college when there was a much more militant feel to it all," she says. "My viewpoint got to be much more that all I wanted to do was make a place that was safe for women to work because it wasn't necessarily safe in a lot of restaurants."

The bakery is not a cooperative, but there's little hierarchy there. No formal job descriptions. Workers have a say in what comes next— and everyone usually has a lot to say. Everyone wears the same blue apron—front or back of house—no uniforms. "The community [of the bakery] is almost as important as the food you take out of here," Penny says. "Everyone picks up on what the attitude is around here. It's friendly, and it's fun, and the food should be good too." She winks at me.

When you work at Ceres Bakery you have to leave the patriarchy-centered ideas of individualistic capitalism you've learned in school or from your family or hometown behind. "There's an education in freedom that occurs here," Penny explains. "The idea of fun in work. The people that flourish are people right on the verge of figuring out who they are. When they learn that a workplace can have this environment, it's an eye-opener."

That sense of community extends to the loyal customers themselves. "My thing was to always make this place be a small, safe environment for anybody in the world to come in here and get the food that they wanted," Penny says. "Everybody has to be treated really fairly because that's the right thing to do." We chat in the back room of the bakery, late afternoon sun streaming through the window where a jade plant sits with a little sign propped on its dirt that reads: *Please don't water me.* While we talk, a worker comes in with a promising paper bag application; someone else steps in to say that the woman who'd locked her keys in her car got them out; someone else sits nearby and says hi; and a counter person saunters up to our table to ask if they make brioche like a bread that someone can fill with custard? Penny says, yes they'd do a loaf, sure. But not those small individual brioches. No way. She turns to me and smiles, her eyes sparkling, her long gray hair coiled up: "Sound familiar?"

I can still call the bakery for advice if I need it. Or more likely, Facebook message everyone so there's a big, rowdy emoji-fest as answers to my questions come in. Back then, when I wasn't working, I hung out there, sitting on the back counter and swinging my legs, or I called in from my apartment nearby to ask where to get the oil changed in my car. Three of the women who were on staff when I worked there still work shifts *twenty-eight years later.*

December 2016, on a lark, I ask Penny if I can work a pre-Christmas rush shift with my old friend and fantastic pie baker Lyn Voss when I fly in to visit my friends Pam and Guy. Pam is sick, and I find myself heading to Portsmouth each month to visit. That night we roll piecrusts, pinch tart crusts, and cut a gazillion top crust stars and laugh and gossip as if I've never left the place. "We always knew you were going to be famous," Lyn says, her muscular arms pushing around the giant rolling pin like it's a twig.

"I'm not famous, Lyn," I say.

"Yeah, yeah," she replies, smiling, flapping a hand in my direction. Flour smudges her apron. Her eyeglasses glint in the bakery light.

These women taught me the practicalities of living a strong and vibrant life on my own terms. They taught me that it's best to have a sense of humor while you educate people in their sexist ways. That it's okay to be butch or femme—whatever you want. But figure out what you want and who you are and go from there. They taught me how to knit, how to pack for a four-day hike, and the value of whole milk and full-fat butter. They nurtured me in every way possible as I labored for three years, working my way nearly full-time through my last two years of undergrad and full-time a year more. Even after I leave for San Francisco, I come back every year, for years, to work shifts when I visit to earn enough gas money to make it back to the West Coast. The night I work with Lyn she reminds me that people come to work at the bakery searching for themselves, and once they do, it's time for them to leave. The long-haulers are happy to watch us go out into the world. They know what role they play. Penny and Lyn make change on a long arc, and quietly, confidently, slowly, the world becomes a better place, one scattered former employee at a time.

To this day I feel the bakery is my home and the people who worked there with me are my family, but I don't live in Portsmouth. I had to leave, just like I once had to stay. Portsmouth got smaller and smaller, and one day it was too small for me. I didn't know I needed a city, but I did. So I got into a car with my long-haired boyfriend and headed west, living out of that car for three months until we hit another coast and found a room to rent, then an apartment, in San Francisco. I stayed in that city for three years, and I learned some more important things about being a woman, a feminist, a writer, and an ex-patriot industrial town survivor. I didn't know it then, but I was circling back, like a homing pigeon on a long run. San Francisco to Lincoln, Nebraska. Lincoln, Nebraska, to Pittsburgh, Pennsylvania. After years of reckoning, I was finding a way back into a place I had to find my way out of.

THE WORST
POSSIBLE OFFENSE

The fall of 1991, as my boyfriend and I drove from New Hampshire to Pennsylvania to Virginia to West Virginia to Vermont and then all along the northern route through Michigan, Wisconsin, Minnesota, North Dakota, Montana, Idaho, Washington, Oregon, and California, the one consistent thing we witnessed from town to town and city to city was an aqua blue poster with a naked baby boy splayed out and floating underwater in a swimming pool, staring straight at the camera, his little penis just in view, grabbing for a dollar bill spiked by a fish hook.

It was, of course, the promo image for the band Nirvana's album *Nevermind.* The now iconic swimming baby gazed at us from the window of every record store, everywhere we went—towns and cities, big and small. The band had just moved from the indie darling label Sub Pop to the major American label DGC Records. And although the album wasn't expected to be a blockbuster, it took the United States by storm and yanked grunge from underground to aboveground. Fast, like a slouching, chain-smoking superhero.

That fall, every time my boyfriend saw that floating baby poster he'd point and mumble, "Sellouts," pushing his long, straight hair out of his face, adjusting his vintage mohair sweater.

Because I was traveling before the world was globally connected by the internet—no swipes, no clicks, no cell phones, laptops, or iPads—destinations remained isolated from each other. I had been part of an arts scene in the Boston area that didn't really understand there were other fully formed alternative cultures thriving in other cities. It wasn't until I rolled into Minneapolis, Chicago, Seattle, and Portland on this trip that I started to understand in a specific way that there were underground alternative music, art, and writing scenes thriving in unison, but not necessarily identically. We would very soon be called Generation X and slackers and other lethargic-sounding lingo-ed names—Douglas Coupland and Richard Linklater had just published and released their 1991 novel and movie respectively.

As Reagan and then Bush pulled the United States back toward the tight, conservative values of the 1950s, and into what we saw as senseless wars, many young people bowed out, got in their cars, and drove. Of course, I didn't understand this context in the summer of 1991. All I knew was that I wanted up and out—of everything.

I call them the Feral Years. It was a time of exile for me. From my family and many of my friends. I don't know why I needed to leave, to go, to enter into many worlds I didn't know or understand, but I did. What came of it is I grew to know the United States as not a single place but a country with many "countries" within it—all with distinct cultures and rules of appropriate behavior.

The collective definition of our generation was coming, but the labels hadn't been glued into place yet. On the road we ran into each other in state parks, at bars and clubs and diners. We were easy to recognize—flannel shirts, thrift-store dresses, Doc Martens, faded jeans, and vintage eyeglass frames. We had dropped out—but we weren't calling it that. We weren't as deliberate as the Lost Generation and the Boomers before us. We just sort of weaseled our way under mainstream culture because there was nothing up there that appealed to us.

Nevermind was released into the world on September 24, 1991, the exact same September we decided to travel the country. We left on September 16 of that year. I wrote in my journal that day: "And so it begins. The end of a nice safe life in Portsmouth and the beginning of something very uncertain." By November 23 of the same year, just about the time we were landing in San Francisco, "Smells Like Teen Spirit," the now-hit single, climbed to #1 on the Billboard charts, as Kurt Cobain grungily told us over car speakers, transistor radios, and stereo systems that it was less dangerous with the lights out.

By the time we moved into our first apartment in the then-so-very-not-yet-gentrified Hayes Valley neighborhood of San Francisco in January 1992, *Nevermind* had sold three million copies, and although grunge had just been born into the mainstream of America, it was dead to us.

"There are no brakes on the hype at this point. It's just going through the roof," Bruce Pavitt, co-owner of Seattle's Sub Pop Records, told Michael Azerrad for *Rolling Stone* magazine on April 16, 1992. "Seattle is a relatively isolated northern city with heavy precipitation and little to do except drink beer and jam in the basement," Azerrad observed, shedding light on Seattle's day-to-day before the rise of Microsoft, Starbucks, and Amazon.

Grunge's heyday came, to a great degree, from my generation's relaxed discontent, simmering frustration, and ongoing boredom. Mark Arm from the Sub Pop band Mudhoney, concurred, saying the Seattle scene formed out of "two *i's*: isolation and inbreeding." But the guitar was out of the case by '92. *Time, Entertainment Weekly,* and *USA Today* covered the Northwest scene like anthropologists discovering a lost civilization.

By November 15, 1992, grunge fashion had hit the front page of the *New York Times* style section. James Truman, the editor of *Details* magazine seemed to be the only one looking at it honestly: "To me the thing about grunge is it's not anti-fashion, it's un fashion. Punk was anti-fashion. It made a statement. Grunge is about not making a statement, which is why it's crazy for it to become a fashion statement," he told Rick Marin.

It doesn't matter that I now think *Nevermind* is brilliant and that I now feel the music itself does reflect all of the fury and restlessness of my generation; it doesn't matter that I get weepy nostalgic when I hear the song "Smells Like Teen Spirit." None of that matters. We wouldn't have gone to see Nirvana play on that trip if someone had given us free tickets. Why? Because they were sellouts, and we were not.

Who were not (yet) sellouts? Babes in Toyland playing in their own city at the club First Avenue in Minneapolis on October 7, 1991. Kat Bjelland dressed in a trampy-cute baby-doll dress, sing-screamed at us from the stage, and we sucked it in.

Writing for the *New York Times* in 1992 Karen Schoemer called Bjelland's voice "loud, brutal and vitriolic. It's not very ladylike, and it's not at all pretty." We'd heard that sometimes Prince showed up at the club. We clutched bottles of beer, stuffed toilet paper in our ears, and watched these messy-haired women in polyester thrift-store dresses, tights, Mary Jane shoes, and lace scream and bang and thump in a style that Schoemer called "aggressively amateurish." Then we drove my car to a rest area outside of Minneapolis and slept in it until daybreak—our sleep intermittently interrupted by a bunch of high school kids who'd landed at the rest stop to yell and throw bottles for a while.

Back then we had a whole pile of AAA maps, and the beauty of these maps was that they designated all of the rest areas along the routes. This was our strategy for "staying" in cities where we didn't know anyone. My boyfriend stretched out on the front seat, me in the back—all our stuff crammed into the car's trunk. In the morning we could wash up in the bathrooms and make breakfast on our portable gas stove at the picnic table kiosks.

Kurt Cobain and I were born in the same year: 1967. I didn't admire Nirvana. I preferred five other bands that could have made it big instead of them but didn't choose to do so. The point was, of course, that no one wanted to make it big. Making it big meant you'd sold out, and selling out was the worst possible offense you could make in our world.

To stay underground and undercover while still remaining true to your art was the goal. Albeit a self-defeating goal in a capitalist society—it was the goal nonetheless. "In the nineties, the worst insult you could lob—or get—was to be a *sellout*," Rebecca Schuman writes in her 2018 *Longreads* essay "You've Reached the Winter of Our Discontent," where she deftly examines the cultural legacy of Gen X, a generation that she claims "refuses to age gracefully." She continues, "Dominant mass-produced mainstream culture—literally anything, the exact moment it became popular enough to no longer be confined to your friend's basement and maybe a 'zine—deserved to be mocked. If you were lucky enough to like something before it got big, then you found yourself flush with the only currency Gen X accepted." This currency, Schuman notes, is a kind of cool, a cool that couldn't be touched by commercialization because as soon as it was, it was no longer cool anymore.

We traveled for three months. I kept immaculate spending records and would not let my boyfriend buy more than ten albums total at used stores across the country. This was the topic of most of our arguments at the time. We couldn't purchase any single item of thrift-store clothing over three dollars. I was neurotically focused on the fact that we would not end up like many of our friends, who started on trips and then had to turn back because they'd run out of money halfway through. We were going to be creative and victorious.

We stayed in one motel for one night near the end of the trip, in Oregon—the rest of the time we snuck into campgrounds, crashed on friends' couches, and slept in rest areas. We made it to San Francisco, into a one-month one-room sublet in a friend's shared apartment with one hundred dollars left to our names.

I charted our course in my journal: neon signs at dusk on small-town streets, the "big, wide sky" over Lake Superior, spaces filled with "air and sunlight and wide, low towns, unobtrusive on my time or space," and "distant gunfire because duck season started today" in Minnesota. We hit the Badlands and witnessed its "soupy dried up rivers of tan and rock formations with tube sock stripes of rose and gold." We saw prairie dogs and buffalo and heard coyotes and their chanting howling at night. And when we hit San Francisco I wrote, "I feel lost. It's too big. It's too something. It's not dirty enough. This place."

The day after we arrived in San Francisco my boyfriend signed up with Olsten Temporary Services and got a two-week job, and I followed suit. We found a studio apartment and signed a lease that would start January 1. We drove back to New Hampshire in a now infamous trip with another couple in two cars, and I charted the route, designating where we would meet up every so many miles at the first "place" on the right, but I didn't understand the changing scale of the state maps in the Rand McNally atlas, so things got a little strange.

We rented a tiny U-Haul trailer, got into an argument that would continue off and on for the next three years because my non-musician boyfriend wanted to bring his guitar and amp along as essential items, picked up my cat Nicki, who had been staying with a friend, and hit the road again—this time in late December. We were forced down to the southern route by the time we hit Nebraska because of raging snowstorms and black ice. Nicki seemed to love New Mexico, although she did not love the road trip and foamed at the mouth and howled for four days straight. But once we were settled into our studio apartment and called in our availability to the agency, we started temping again.

This compulsion to leave, to be moving *away from* seemed to be a kind of anti-nesting that my body and brain took seriously in these years. There are a zillion stories of this type—the most well-known twentieth-century incarnation being Jack Kerouac's 1957 *On the Road*. But also, for me: Robert M. Pirsig's *Zen and the Art of Motorcycle Maintenance*, and *Blue Highways* by William Least Heat-Moon. These stories about men leaving and discovering America while finding themselves weren't an exact fit for a twenty-four-year-old woman, but I read them, and I, too, wanted to eat apple pie while getting lost in America.

Of course, it was never just the men who left or wanted to leave the conscripted lives America had dictated to them. The men were just the ones given ink space to tell their reckless stories. "Those of us who flew out the door had no usable models for what we were doing," writes Joyce Johnson in her 1994 foreword to her 1983 book *Minor Characters*, which chronicles her life in the beat scene of the late 1950s, particularly with Kerouac, who was her boyfriend off and on for several years. "We did not want to be our mothers or our spinster schoolteachers or the hard-boiled career women depicted on screen. And no one had taught us how to be women artists or writers," she writes.

As I read her foreword and the chapters that followed while sitting in my Pittsburgh living room in 2018, Johnson brought to life a nostalgic unrest that felt familiar to me. I could sense the same compulsion to escape joining us across decades. It was a kind of drive, like a sex drive, and at the time it didn't feel like it would ever have an end.

Johnson talks of the "girl gangs," the forgotten groups of women who, like their famous boy gang counterparts (Kerouac, Ginsberg, Corso, Frank), left conventional America in the dust. "There was a restlessness in everyone I knew," Johnson writes about her women friends in the fall of 1956. As *On the Road* finally neared publication in 1957, she sensed "the 'bottled eagerness' of the fifties was about to be uncorked." She suspected "thousands were waiting for a prophet to liberate them from the cautious middle-class lives they had been reared to inherit."

On April 20, 1993, my friend Charlyn and I set out on a San Francisco-to-New Hampshire-to-Oregon road trip that we chronicled in a collaborative journal. Charlyn rediscovered that journal in her (still working) 1984 stinkbug-brown Vanagon—named the Ark—in the summer of 2017, as she got the vehicle up and going for yet another cross-country trip. This time with her long-time partner Mark. They live in Corvallis, Oregon, these days.

She was part of the early '90s migration from Portsmouth to the West Coast. She landed in Portland, Oregon, but before that had been a baker with me at Ceres Bakery while finishing a master's degree in American history. She's now a high school English teacher. In 2017 they stopped in Pittsburgh, where I live now, and in an homage to many of our trips together, the Ark broke down for a day or two.

Looking through the journal together jolted me back to a time and place when we explored for exploration's sake any chance we could get. "You do not take a trip; a trip takes you," is written in colorful orange marker and bordered by little drawings of vines and flowers in yellow, purple, and green inside the front cover in my handwriting.

It looks like one of us bought the journal in San Francisco's Chinatown. It has a Kelly green border bound in a maroon silk fabric print that sports pagodas, a blooming tree, and some horses. The spine reads DIARY in gold script. We wrote inside the cover that if the journal was found it should be sent to Ceres Bakery, where neither of us had worked for years.

By April 22 we'd made it through Tahoe, ate fish tacos, and already fixed a Vanagon sparkplug issue with a wrench borrowed from our waitress's boyfriend in a K-Mart parking lot. We missed the sunset in Death Valley because of this. My first entry is a Rilke quote: "Do not now seek the answers which cannot be given you because you would not be able to live them. And the point is to live everything. *Live* the questions now. Perhaps you will then gradually, without noticing it, live along some distant day into the answer."

We experienced a lot of headwinds, drank a lot of tea, spotted prairie dogs along Route 66 at 11:30 a.m., and loved Albuquerque, particularly Fred's coffee shop. We watched the moon grow golden and set behind us. We spotted one, two, and eventually eleven old men wearing feed caps in a diner in Oklahoma. There was a brick silo painted like a Budweiser can outside Bloomer, Arkansas. Charlyn lost her wallet—we returned for the wallet; a nice man named Joe was working at Sun Recording Studio. We bought donuts at Fox's Donut Den in Nashville; we felt out of place or "not from here" everywhere we went, even though we decided to wear baseball caps to better fit in. We visited Graceland, and our tour guide looked like Donny Osmond, and he told us in a quiet aside that he'd just been to the gay pride parade in San Francisco.

At a stop in my hometown, Beaver Falls, Pennsylvania, my dad gave us a tire gauge and decided while gazing out at the Ark parked in his driveway, one leg up on a kitchen chair, arms folded across his chest, that road trips are "good for self-confidence and leadership skills."

We hit New England just in time to meet our friends at the Press Room bar in Portsmouth and for Charlyn to attend a wedding, and then we were on the road again. By May 13 we were back to sagebrush and feed caps outside of Paxton, Illinois, then we hit Wyoming where we spent two nights in the back room of a mechanic's shop in Laramie. Claus the mechanic got a whole dozen cookies sent to him once we were home. The Ark got a new clutch.

Then as we noticed it no longer smelled like cows, we hit the sign that at the time meant home for both of us: San Francisco / Salt Lake City Route 80—Portland Route 84. Driving through Utah "there is constantly changing low and high mountains, turbulent brown streams, thin green valleys." Later that night at a diner, a woman walked in wearing "cowboy boots, a flowered hip hugging cotton skirt, white cotton sleeveless blouse." She swung her hips, and when the waitress said, "Bathroom's that way," the woman replied to the room, "I'm not looking for a bathroom. I'm looking for a *man.*" Then she swung back out the door past the classic revolving pie display. We wanted to be her.

We slept beneath stars and trees for another free night, and then in our last entry it was 6:20 a.m., and we were 158 miles from Portland. I'm not entirely sure how I got home to San Francisco, but the trip officially ended on May 16—thirty-one days after it started, the heat stuck on high in the Ark the entire time.

Eventually I turned from temping back to baking at Sally's Bakery in Potrero Hill. And that's where I was midmorning on April 8, 1994—finishing up an overnight baking shift—when Jenny, the bakers' unanimously least favorite counterperson, came in crying. She immediately turned off the jazz station I had going and told me, as the bakery rang in silence, that Kurt Cobain was dead. And although he had been dead to me for years, I did feel a pang of loss. Something I would understand on a much greater scale in later years. He was of our generation, and our generation was small. We couldn't afford to lose much.

Jenny was years younger than I and came at Nirvana from a much different angle. Kurt Cobain represented something to her—someone who had made it on his own terms, perhaps. An MTV legend? Nevertheless, on this day she first would not let any music of any kind be played in our tiny bakery space, and then she was so inconsolable that she was sent home. I worked the register until my roommate Christopher, who also worked at Sally's Bakery, could bus in to pick up her hours.

I stayed to hang out for a while. We turned the jazz station back on, and neither of us recalls talking too much about Kurt Cobain that day at all, except Chris relaying the rumor that Courtney Love was walking around Capital Hill asking people trivia questions about Kurt and giving away all of his things.

My first semester of graduate school years later, poet Professor Greg Kuzma gave me an anthology called *Drive, They Said: Poems about Americans and Their Cars*, edited by Kurt Brown. This is how I came to think about my behind-the-wheel experience in empowered feminist terms. In the poem "Driving to Houston" Linda Gregg writes:

> At three in the morning I go through
> a place where red and green traffic
> lights shine against the swarthy sky
> while a black man rides his bicycle
> along the empty street. The houses
> dark and no place open to eat.

The allure of the road trip is these stealth moments of observation. The freedom to drive through a silent street, to control your destination. The strength of movement and travel.

I came to understand the historic power that came with a woman's legal right to drive, something both Gertrude Stein and Edith Wharton write about. Of her "motor-flights," Wharton says, "Above all these recovered pleasures must be ranked the delight of taking a town unawares, stealing on it by back ways and unchronicled paths, and surprising in it some aspect of past time, some silhouette hidden for half a century or more by the ugly mask of railway embankments and the iron bulk of a huge station."

In *The Autobiography of Alice B. Toklas*, Stein writes, "Gertrude Stein always says that she only has two real distractions, pictures and automobiles." Stein's first car was named Auntie, her second Godiva. She drove for the American Fund for the French Wounded during World

War I, although she never learned to drive in reverse. The power and freedom she felt while driving is reflected in many photographs of Stein, boldly behind the wheel, Alice B. Toklas as passenger. The act of turning a key, pressing the gas pedal, placing two hands on the wheel, the horizon in your sights, became everything for me.

When I think about these years of exile, living in an eccentric West Coast city that had not yet exploded into tech-bro gentrification, traveling with no real destination, working hours that gave me time to explore, I realize that this time formed the core of my aesthetic. It helped guide me in the future to find the kind of happiness I needed to have a productive creative life. It helped me understand how to empower and free myself behind the wheel. It taught me the joy of being frugal. The importance of friendship. How essential it was to know how to cook and bake one's own food. The release from consumer society that came with that kind of living beneath the mainstream.

I did not have much anxiety or fear in those years. I hadn't yet experienced stress or career-numbing pressure. I didn't necessarily know who I was, but I knew I wanted to be a writer, and it seemed to me that being in the world, experiencing the world, exiling myself into the unknown, was one key to success that had nothing to do with selling out.

FAITH IN MOVEMENT

Riverview United Methodist Church is perched at the top of Eleventh Street Hill in Patterson Township. It's a sturdy brick building with two red doors and a marquee in the front, a parking lot in the rear. Inside, red carpeting leads down the aisle to an altar, which has a simple gold cross paired with a candle on each side, seating for a choir, and a pipe organ to the right. Plain, blonde wooden pews fill the airy space, and simple stained glass windows border the sanctuary. In my childhood, during the warm months when the sermon is in progress and the windows are open, a person sitting on the far left of the pew can hear cars whooshing by on Darlington Road and non-church-going kids thumping balls on their way to the basketball courts at the elementary school. I attend this church nearly every Sunday growing up.

I grew up in Patterson Township, a borough nestled on a bluff just above Beaver Falls, Pennsylvania, a mill town like you read about when you read about mill towns. Yet I'm not devoted to this Rustbelt place in the way movies like *The Deer Hunter* would want you to believe me to be. But I am of Beaver Falls, because I grew up there, and union culture is Rustbelt culture whether you're directly in it or not.

Beaver Falls, Pennsylvania—the birthplace of football legend Joe Namath and home to rocker Donnie Iris—is part of a packed lineup of communities along the Ohio and then Beaver Rivers that lead away from or into Pittsburgh depending on your perspective. Beaver Falls, New Brighton, Beaver, Monaca, Baden, Aliquippa, and Ambridge were historically dependent upon the riverways for transportation and industry.

The city itself was founded in 1868, and because of clay, gas, coal, and ore reserves, it attracted waves of industry: cutlery, glass, pottery, and steel. Seventh Avenue, the city's main street, is wide. Rumor has it that settlers made it big enough to turn a team of horses around without backing up. When you stand at the upper end and look down the street, you can visualize that Beaver Falls was once regal, bustling, and filled with active storefronts and multilevel department stores, the way it was when my parents first moved here. A train line and trolley once connected it to Pittsburgh and surrounding towns. In 1950, seventeen thousand people lived in Beaver Falls. Today there are around nine thousand.

We want stories to be easy, but they aren't. And this is part of my conundrum as I look to define home. My parents came from Appalachian farming roots to live in a place where they didn't have relatives working in the mill, where they made their own way, not working in the mill. They were outsiders among outsiders who became insiders in their community. I'm an outsider by association. I took that part to heart.

Before I was born, my family—although religious—often didn't go to church because they were heading home each weekend to Tionesta, Pennsylvania, located along the Allegheny River in Forest County, where their extended families lived. "We'd developed a habit different than everyone else," my dad says.

By the time I came into the picture, they were pretty much weekly churchgoers. I was a fanciful and interior child and listened closely to the sermons. I was always keen for a good story, but the Bible, except for the beautiful writing in Genesis, bored me. I came to equate Jesus with other make-believe characters that my parents introduced me to: Santa Claus, the Easter Bunny, the Tooth Fairy. I came to believe very early on that no one believed any of it was real. I was obviously wrong about that on some counts, but it took me a long time to figure that out.

Sometimes on Sundays when I was little, instead of church we made the trek to Tionesta for the huge McWilliams family reunion or a wedding or a baby shower for the Flicks. The drive and the visit took the place of worship—they seemed to zero each other out in my parents' minds, a kind of exile and return story, biblically satisfying in the ritualistic nature of it all. And maybe it's this driving that I came to associate with worship, as in later years I became a disciple of the road trip in every form.

Since my two brothers are much older than I, they were already off in their adult lives, driving their families to Tionesta in their own cars or not joining in. It was almost like being an only child, spending long periods of time alone in the backseat, in the magical realism of my imagination, as my father's Cadillac snaked along highways and back roads inching toward their rural beginnings, the a.m. radio station screeching and squawking the Pirates baseball game as we veered in and out of reception.

In 1949, the same year Andy Warhola boards a passenger train in Downtown Pittsburgh bound for New York City, my fourteen-year-old dad loses his nickname, Popeye, and moves with his family from Allegany, New York, to Leeper, Pennsylvania. There, they live in a place on Jack Callahan's farm with an outhouse, hand-pumped water, and coal heat. The war is over. Arthur Miller's *Death of a Salesman* premieres on Broadway. The Yankees win the World Series, jazz blasts at Birdland, George Orwell publishes *1984*, ten million televisions are warming up in people's homes, and the first rocket launches in a fit of smoke in Cape Canaveral, Florida. Prosperity dominates the U.S. narrative. It plays out in shiny new ad campaigns, and *someone* has to illustrate them.

Pittsburgh in 1949 is just barely beginning to deal with its pollution, lack of downtown infrastructure, and reputation. "Both the Pennsylvania and the B. & O. set the visitor down near the so-called Golden Triangle, the business center where low-hanging smog and smudgy dust perpetuate the tradition of Pittsburgh dirt," Al Hine writes in 1949. Hine, a Pittsburgh ex-patriot, scored a twenty-one-page cover story for October's edition of *Holiday* magazine. Packed with both full-page color spreads and black-and-white photos, the feature showcases the city's history, grit, industrialists, cosmopolitan chic, and working class. "It has all the usual urban contrasts," Hine writes, "wealth and slums, culture and ignorance, high ideals and intolerance."

Images that accompany the article: workers in long white coats box gas meters at Rockwell Manufacturing, where my mom and Aunt Doris will find secretarial jobs four years later; a neon J&L Steel sign glows at dusk; George Pavlic, a young laborer and war veteran, works a dangerously hot job as a high mill plugger at the McKeesport National Tube Company; he drinks beer with friends at Mickey's, smiles at his date at Bill Green's dine, dance, and drinkery, and attends a CIO-USA meeting with a hearty group of men; his parents are freshly minted Americans who immigrated from Yugoslavia; a framed print of Jesus on the cross hangs above their dining table beside what looks like a high school diploma.

In the final pages of the feature, a young mom smiles in silhouette. Her hair neatly curled, she wears a simple belted dress and sandals as she holds the hand of a toddler. The child stretches to make the next tread of a set of wooden city steps. They're midway up. Seventy-five steep treads with four landings, and the picture doesn't capture the whole staircase.

The Pittsburgh my parents move to in 1953 is the eighth largest city in the United States. They stay for three years. It has trolley cars, 677,000 people, and factories operating at full tilt. The Greater Pittsburgh Airport was built in 1952. The Alcoa Building rises in 1953. By 1954 Jonas Salk, working at the University of Pittsburgh, has started field trials on his polio vaccine. Pittsburgh is in the midst of its first renewal called Renaissance I. Some extremely modest pollution controls are enacted that turn the sky from ever-present smoky soot to regular Pittsburgh overcast gray; J&L mill expands. The shiny, chromium steel Gateway Center buildings loom, and the Point becomes the official triangular entrance to the city as Pittsburgh reorients itself to its three rivers. The Hill District, Pittsburgh's bustling mixed-race neighborhood with its hopping jazz scene, sees its devastating demise to make way for the Civic Arena.

Andy Warhola, like me, believes in the gospel of movement, of get-up-and-go. As he leaves Pittsburgh and chugs along the Pennsylvania countryside, rounding the famous horseshoe curve in the Allegheny Mountains near Altoona, then across the Susquehanna and Delaware Rivers, east to Philadelphia, and north to New York, the *a* drops from his last name and rolls down a steep hill.

Pittsburgh is the dot on the map in Allegheny County that I drive away from as I head into Beaver County on route 376. First zipping along dense urban streets, then a series of confusing bypasses, then through the Fort Pitt Tunnel and past Robinson Town Center's plaza malls and big box stores, and out to the highway along densely wooded slopes and rock ridges that have been carved through to make what I grew up calling "The Big Road."

In the spring and summer there are purple and yellow pockets of wildflowers here and there. Dead deer, possums, and raccoons line the side of the road. A deep organic smell rises up beyond it all, a combination of earth and rain. With the windows down I hear crickets and locusts wailing in and out of range, and the air smells warm. It's distinct—the way this smell nestles into me and the air permeates my skin. In the fall, there are bright bursts of leaves along the hillsides in red, burgundy, yellow, and brown. In winter, fat snowflakes layer themselves down to cover patches of black ice.

The second half of the drive passes Pittsburgh International Airport. For years it signals I'm about to hit ground zero when traveling home from out of state, sitting in the passenger seat after one parent or another has fetched me from the airport. I watch the familiar tree-lined rock formations zip past, anticipating gauging the obvious ways I've changed since the previous visit home. I look forward to regressing in the TV room, eating Snyder's potato chips with french onion dip, and sneaking M&Ms from the bowl my mother always has filled on the kitchen counter. I don't look forward to leaving the progressive communities I live in, to explaining why I don't eat margarine or meat, or why I won't be moving back.

All the years I travel home from afar, the one thing I can count on is Beaver Falls remaining exactly the same—dead, down, and out. It's as if each year I return to 1985 again, like *Groundhog Day* meets *All the Right Moves*. Every visit. This rubber-band experience has me stretching further away between each visit and pinging back, shockingly to where I started from.

This day it's 2017. My dad leans back in his office chair at Flick Financial, an investment firm he started with my brother Dan and two of my nephews after working for MetLife for sixty years. Patient in his speech and determined and steady in his gait, my dad intertwines his hands on his belly when he gets deeper into a story, which can take a while to tell.

He's eighty-two as of June and, although technically retired, still comes to work nearly every day in a suit and tie to serve as a consultant to the business. He's wearing a tan jacket, brown pants, a lighter tan shirt, and a tie festooned with repeating Rotary Club logos. A family portrait sits on the filing cabinet along with a black-and-white photo of me and my two brothers taken back when I was in college. We're laughing, leaning on an old train trestle in Beaver, Pennsylvania. Lining one wall is a sampling of the many sales awards he has earned throughout his long, successful career. A Century Club Award for lifetime achievement and other engraved plaques make a sturdy grid.

Today, where I live in the South Side Slopes of Pittsburgh, everything I need is downhill: post office, grocery store, restaurants, and library. I lace up and walk down. It's the walking up that reminds me I've chosen to live in an unlikely place. As I pump up the steep city steps, I'm reminded it doesn't matter how good of shape a person is in; they're panting by the time they make it to my front door.

Pittsburgh is hilly however you traverse it, but I live up in the boonies. For the most part, the little, densely packed houses that terrace the steep hillside aren't fancy, and our roads weren't really made for modern cars or two-way traffic. But we make it work.

The South Side Slopes has sixty-eight sets of city steps that bind together its streets and alleyways and rows of houses, which stack up the hill like colorful 3D wallpaper. The hillside is often photographed, less often visited. Some streets are paper streets—steps and trails that stand in for real streets on the map where roads have never gone. Although the City of Pittsburgh is technically in charge of maintaining the public steps because they're considered infrastructure like bridges and roads, the general attitude from Public Works in past years has been to ignore the steps until something crumbles (concrete) or breaks (wood).

In general we're pretty okay with being ignored up here in our fantastically unrealistic urban landscape. If we had a Slopes motto it might read: *We're Fine. Leave Us Alone.* This motto extends to home renovations, disputes between neighbors, parking rules, and who has the unspoken right-of-way on a one-lane two-way street. (The car coming down has the right-of-way on Sterling Street; the car driving up has the right-of-way on Barry.) There's an air of the wild West up here on our unreasonable hills. For people like me, it's certainly part of the attraction.

In a Pittsburgh History and Landmarks Foundation lecture, "The Mathematics of Style and Taste," architectural historian Charles Rosenblum argues that architecture is an analogy for the human body. The steep city steps all around Pittsburgh reflect both the grit of the laborers and also the challenge of the working class. "We tell stories in shapes," Rosenblum says. The city steps are an open book, and their theme has something to do with impossibility, something to do with pain, with stretching just a bit more to arrive somewhere unexpected.

We tell stories in shapes. When I learn that Andy Warhol may have taken a Greyhound bus to New York City instead of the train, I feel a seismic shift in how I've understood the world. No horseshoe curve? No *a* tumbling down the hill? No conductor in a snazzy cap snipping his ticket?

Everyone says that Andy Warhol took the train to New York. It's how the story goes. The poet Gerald Stern claims to have been the one to drive him to the train (not bus) station. He says they got ice cream beforehand. But a Greyhound makes more sense, really. It would have been cheaper than the train. And the bus's gleaming, dreamy curves would have signaled the new shiny world that lured Warhol in, a world he would help define.

The Carnegie Museum of Art's website says he took a Greyhound. Who am I to argue? But the shape of the story says the train. This is why facts are nearly never exactly right. Warhol took himself to New York City after being formed by the city of Pittsburgh. He grew up poor and soon would be rich. I don't know if he believed in the American dream the way my mother and father did when they moved to Pittsburgh from Tionesta, driving a 1941 Pontiac, but he believed in soup and factories and holding back to lurk in the corner at parties. He believed in God and Shirley Temple. He believed in testing the shape of a room. He believed in making it. And he did.

The entire time I live in Beaver Falls, the highway, The Big Road, also known locally as Parkway West/East (even though it isn't labeled as such on any sign, and the road runs North/South) ends at my hometown exit: Chippewa. It just stops. A dystopian dead end, the road itself serving as a metaphor for the region's eventual, grand fall from industrial grace. Grass grows beyond the paved highway, and all cars exit at Chippewa like obedient ducklings searching for water.

The Parkway extension was completed in the '90s, so the driving experience isn't quite as dramatic today. Now Chippewa is just—as multiple signs warn—"the last exit before the toll road."

My high school friend Mary Brice calls Beaver Valley—the industrial mecca that history hails—a figment of our imaginations. It's hard to remember a place that disappeared before your eyes. My memories are blips. There's a bustling downtown filled with shops and shoppers and then it's closed up and empty. Poof.

My middle school English teacher, Michael Moore, remembers how the shift looked from behind his desk. "It was really weird teaching at a place where the mills were running 24/7 to virtually nothing with no transition," he tells me via email. "Beaver Falls went from a thriving downtown business [district] to what you imagine Beirut to look like." I had Mr. Moore for English in 1980, where he wore crazy ties and we acted out scenes from *Watership Down*, and then he moved to Blackhawk High School at the same time I did, where he continued to wear the ties as he taught my first ever creative writing class.

Until he boards that train or bus out of Pittsburgh, Andy Warhola, for sure, attends St. John Chrysostom Byzantine Catholic Church in "The Run" of Greenfield, a working-class neighborhood that would be called a holler or hollow in some parts of the country, as it's nestled at the base of a bluff between the Oakland, Greenfield, and Hazelwood neighborhoods. Steep city steps can lead a person out and in.

St. John's is set up above a residential sidewalk. It's built of cream-colored bricks and has tall spires that point into the Pittsburgh sky. Adorning each spire is a dome, and punctuating each dome is a cross with three horizontal spikes. Once inside, the church's interior fills with glam and gilding. The walls are a deep mustard yellow with accents of salmon, and there are stylized gold stars painted within a deep blue background inside the hollow of the dome above the altar.

The poet Peter Oresick invites me to join him one Sunday after services. Like Warhol, Peter comes from Carpatho-Rusyn roots, and although at one point his mother claimed the Oresick family was distantly related to the Warholas, it isn't true. He tells me to bring my camera, that it'll be fun for me to poke around inside.

Along with the intense color of the interior, floor-to-ceiling icons line the walls framed in ornate white woodwork. These images, along with the ritual and incense and otherworldly vibe during the service, would have been stunning, such a contrast to Warhol's day-to-day Pittsburgh world outside the doors: dull, gray polluted skies and litter-strewn walkways.

The Warholas walk to church each Sunday as a family from their house on Dawson Street, and Andy also attends church daily with his mother, Julia. The congregation of St. John's is made up of Carpatho-Rusyn immigrants—Slovaks—exiled from Czechoslovakia, Poland, and Russia. It's Byzantine Catholic, not to be confused with Roman Catholic.

"A heightened veneration is accorded the visual image [in the Byzantine church], the religious icon, which engages the viewer, having a function equivalent to that of scripture," writes Jane Daggett Dillenberger in *The Religious Art of Andy Warhol*, "for the icon mediates between the believer and the holy person represented by the icon." In other words, when people in this church kiss the displayed icons, they believe they are making direct contact with the divine. They are kissing God when they kiss these paintings.

These bright, colorful, iconic images, replicated and towering to the ceiling in Warhol's sanctuary, aren't just a representation of the holy, they're the connection to the holy in the tradition of Warhol's boyhood faith. I find it a very short step from them to his artwork, especially his repeating screen prints of Elvis, Marilyn Monroe, Elizabeth Taylor, Mick Jagger, Muhammad Ali, and Mao. They are the twentieth-century icons in his life, lining the walls in their yellow, pink, green, and purple glory, waiting for the kiss that connects them directly to Pop.

Little-known fact: after Warhol moved to New York City he continued to attend worship services. "As fellow parishioners will remember, he made a point of dropping in on his local church, St. Vincent Ferrer, several days a week until shortly before he died," John Richardson notes in his 1987 eulogy for Warhol. Throughout his adult life, Warhol wore a crucifix, carried a prayer book and rosary, and volunteered regularly at a soup kitchen serving the homeless. "The knowledge of this secret piety inevitably changes our perception of an artist who fooled the world into believing that his only obsessions were money, fame, glamour, and that he was cool to the point of callousness," Richardson continues.

"My Catholic thingy" is how Warhol talked about his religion. His religious practice was a Pittsburgh thing that he imported to New York through his pop culture icons and his own versions of the *Last Supper* (an image that hung above his own childhood dining table) along with the idea of factories. And of course his mother Julia, who came to live with him as soon as he could afford his own apartment, collaborated with him on early design elements and stayed for years until just before her own passing.

Otherwise, it seems Warhol doesn't look back. He stays in touch with family, but not with the city that grew him. He isn't a prodigal son until after his untimely death at age fifty-eight. He doesn't return to Pittsburgh except to be buried. He's a hyper-cool, hip, scene-setting, androgynous, gay New York artist pushing boundaries, hanging with eccentrics and junkies at his factory and exclusive clubs, raking in commissions for portraits, collecting antiques, and all the while sliding this and that into cardboard box time capsules labeled and stored away for who knows what purpose.

"Forty years later, America has appropriated, domesticated, and / commodified Andy Warhol, especially here in Pittsburgh," Peter Oresick writes in the "Notes" section of his poetry collection *Warhol-o-rama*,

> where his sins are now forgiven and his admirers decorate his grave with soup cans and a golden bridge bears his name and his status as native son is secured by an eight-story, 88,000 square foot, single-artist museum—a veritable Taj Warhol. Unbelievable.

From the service at St. John's, Peter and I walk to Big Jim's, a nondescript brick building with a Virgin Mary nook built into its front at the opposite end of Saline Street. Beer signs light the front door and window. The bar/restaurant had been opportunely located near the now-defunct LTV steel plant in the Hazelwood neighborhood of Pittsburgh. Inside, a painting of Big Jim himself hangs above the cash register. He's broad-shouldered and thick-necked, a guy who certainly looks like he wouldn't take any shit.

Peter and I order breakfast and beer. There's a soft light filtering through the one small high window at the end of the bar, and we talk about Carpatho-Rusyns, Warhol, Peter's brain cancer, and poetry. He grew up in Ford City, Pennsylvania, a small Ukrainian immigrant colony on the Allegheny, moved to the city to attend the University of Pittsburgh, and then settled in, writing and editing twelve books of poetry about the working class, working for the University of Pittsburgh Press, and eventually becoming director of the low-res MFA program at Chatham University. Part of Peter's attraction to St. John's church was the connection to his ethnic roots.

After taking a class with an episcopal priest, Peter started painting icons. Similar to the Byzantine philosophy of kissing the icon, the act of painting is supposed to bring you into spiritual contact with God. At first his work manifested traditional saints, but then he went on to paint his literary icons: Walt Whitman, Emily Dickinson, Edgar Alan Poe, as well as Madonna of the Steel Valley.

When we met up at Big Jim's, Peter's cancer was in remission. He died three years later at age sixty-one, leaving behind many sorrowful fans—family members, friends, colleagues, and acquaintances. He was a quiet and curious person, not so much devotedly religious but devoted to family and history and art and poetry and the working class world in which he was raised, which gave him a solid foundation and the most diligent work ethic I've ever seen in a human. Peter never lost his tether to his birthplace. His wife Stephanie Flom told me that after his death she learned every single one of his passwords was Ford City. Unlike me, it was easy for him to love his homeland. Easy for him to rubber band back and forth.

"What is the state of memory?" the Pittsburgh muralist and professor of architecture Douglas Cooper asks in a lecture at the Carnegie Museum of Art. "How do we replicate the sense of a place by living in that place?" His intricate and detailed mural drawings serve as a kind of map for both the complicated streetscape and the memory of Pittsburgh. City steps are everywhere throughout these drawings, surrealistically steep and winding. In a mural section that depicts the South Side Slopes, the houses and steps slur and blur, replicating a memory of the water that rushed down the hills to form this place, as the valleys were created from water running on plateaus, not from land masses shooting upward. The land here has a memory of being flat. It's a carved place, where I live. Set in its ways. Sculpted and then disrupted first by rivers and then by these steps trying to pull it back together again.

In 1998 my new husband Rick and I drive into Pittsburgh in a rented U-Haul truck. We fall right into a city stalled and stuck in a mid-1980s depression, exactly where I'd left off when I escaped to college in 1985. It's a lesson in how time stands still, how the world advances and retreats in spits and spurts. How the shape of a place is the place. How the water keeps running over the rocks making us sink, even though it looks like hills rising. How faith in movement can become faith in standing still.

It's a game of chess. All these bodies moving through time. Tionesta to Pittsburgh, Pittsburgh to New York City, Ford City to Pittsburgh, Pittsburgh to Beaver Falls. We shift and shift to find our place, our next move, unsure of when and how it will all end. We figure out a faith that manifests as a path, and it's the one we take, and soon it feels like truth.

BANK SHOT

A bar with a pool table rests in my third eye. The table's felt is teal wrapped in ugly brown, wide and sturdy. Cigarette smoke wafts, lifts to the ceiling. The word *feminist* rises from the haze, lingers. The pool table is the bar's heart. *Thump-thump* goes the jukebox. *Thump-thump-thump.*

This isn't a metaphor. It takes bravado to function in a bar decorated with beer posters boasting ample cleavage. I've just walked in with my cowboy boots and jeans, with my bright red T-shirt that reads "Piggily Wiggily" in stark white lettering across my breasts. I wear my leather wallet in my back pocket, and thick black eyeglass frames perch on my nose.

I take off the frames, order a whiskey, and ask for change in quarters from the bartender. There's the low hum of conversation and that smell that comes from years of musty beer mopped and lacquered into the bar's corners. At the pool table, I line the quarters up in their slots, experience the push-pull release of tension as the balls drop and roll. That release *is* the metaphor for my rage, simmering on the back burner, released with a clunk and a rumble as the balls clatter and snap into line. I fit them firmly into the black plastic rack.

How to operate in a bar, how to walk up to a pool table without hesitation. What I wear, how I move, I learned through the osmosis of growing up in Beaver Falls, Pennsylvania. A booming and then not-so-booming and then finally dead steel town. Whether your parents worked in the mill or not, you learned a few things: how to play pool, the lyrics to every Bruce Springsteen song, the talk-yelling banter needed to communicate with the mechanic, the ins and outs of the corner bar, and the nuance of pierogies, square-cut pizza, and oversized fish sandwiches served up by church ladies.

If you're good at pool, which I am, you can garner some respect from the men who grip sweating bottles of beer along the bar top over there. Not catcalling, body-objectifying respect, but instead a nod and a "nice bank shot" respect. A kind of "I see you" respect. A stoic respect that has more to do with power than sex, more to do with skill than what the posters offer. This very specific pool-related niche-respect has transferred to many different geographic locations throughout my lifetime.

When I first moved to Lincoln, Nebraska, the bars there confused me. For the three years prior I had lived in San Francisco, and the cowboy aesthetic was all the rage in the Castro. So the bars in Nebraska looked like gay bars to me, which they weren't. They were cowboy bars, a variation on the steelworker bar I grew up with.

It took me awhile, but I soon understood that when Great Plains farmers got dressed up, they looked like gay men, meaning fit cowboys with tight Wrangler jeans and nice boots and hats and snap-up shirts. It did not mean they were progressive or that the man they stood drinking with was their date. It all worked out in my head eventually.

I moved to Lincoln in 1994 to start a graduate degree in English literature with a thesis in creative writing at the state university. I was funded, so it was the first time in my life I had to introduce myself as a writer—at twenty-seven years old. Prior to this I introduced myself as a student, baker, or temp. I liked having a cover, like Superman with Clark Kent. I was never into walking around in my fiction writer cape, especially because it was totally not cool to take on intellectual airs where I grew up. It took me more than a while to casually say, "I'm a fiction writer" without feeling pretentious. It seems so simple now, but back then a sheen of sweat slicked my body at the idea of it.

I countered this anxiety by obsessively playing eight ball at the quarter tables around town. Liz Champlin, a fellow graduate student, joined me. A petite, southern, badass poet, she learned to play with her uncle in the pool halls of Nashville, Tennessee. She is the one who gave me the Piggily Wiggily T-shirt. It served as a counteroffering to my love of the Hinky Dinky grocery stores on the Great Plains, which, to my disappointment, didn't offer merch.

Neither of us had lived in the Great Plains or anything even close to them before arriving in Lincoln. We both freaked out a little at the big sky and the slow, midwestern ways, the weather, the many, many bugs, and the men who seemed afraid to speak to us. We also freaked out about the staid power structure of the English department, its insulation from the real world, and how most of our cohort didn't seem to go out drinking.

We practiced pool in the afternoon at Yia Yia's pizza place. We drank iced tea and held our hands over the pockets to catch the balls so we could play all afternoon on a few quarters. No one seemed to mind. The thing with Lincoln, and really all of Nebraska, was space. Lots of it. Space to park, space to walk, space inside buildings. Space for your brain to slow down. There was just so much empty air floating around. Yia Yia's was big with tall ceilings and wide wooden floors, and we could hide out in the side room and no one noticed us right out in the open. In this way I got very good at long shots and bank shots, and as classes began and I went deep into various brands of critical theory, I started to call the pool table a feminist arena. By year two of my graduate work it became important for me to teach all of the women creative writers in my program how to play pool. Solids and stripes, bank shots and straight shots, the power and feel of a nice, clean break. The sense of dominance that comes to you when you *mean* to sink a ball instead of doing it by accident. They were all into it. And soon we were a girl grad school gang of writing pool players.

But at night during this first semester, Liz and I drank whiskey and challenged men at the quarter tables around town. Over the smoky tables they almost always tried to cheat us, and we always called them on it. This sometimes ended with Liz yelling, "Fuck you" to someone. Yes, we were angry. Really, really angry about a lot of things we weren't necessarily figuring out, but part of it had to do with the pool table and the assumption that we didn't belong. The assumption that we sucked. That we—say it—played like girls. That tamped-down and ambiguous rage fueled our need to own the table, to own them. The power we lost elsewhere we gained back each night by tag team sinking the eight ball again and again in great drunken rushes of victory.

We walked home to our separate apartments along wide, empty O Street, talking too loud, laughing. My boots followed my long strides with dull clicks on the infinite sidewalk lit by the dim streetlights, flashes of neon here and there, all the way to Twenty-Eighth Street.

The Caribbean Club is the oldest bar in the Upper Keys, puttering along since 1938. Its interior was the inspiration for the 1948 John Huston film *Key Largo*, starring Humphrey Bogart and Lauren Bacall. Its façade was used in the film. For my purposes here, what you need to know is they make stiff drinks, there's a pool table, a chalkboard to write your name on for the next game, and no ferns.

The Caribbean Club in Key Largo, Florida, 2017: the linoleum floor remains perpetually dusty and stretches out toward the door. Beyond the bar there's a landing with Adirondack chairs set up to take in the dazzling sunsets across Blackwater Sound. The bathrooms are simple with good intentions. There's a neon Miller High Life sign hanging near the pool table.

The table is a quarter table. You can stack four quarters on the table's edge to designate that you want the next game whether your name is up on the chalkboard or not. The pool cues are ratty and not very straight, but that's okay because that's what I've learned to play with. The table slants a little, and that slope is what I need to figure out if I want to keep playing.

The bartender is not hip or an artisan. He wears a T-shirt and shorts. It looks like he's just methodically serving drinks and making small talk, but he knows what's going on in front and behind him at all times. If trouble brews, he's on it, but you may not know it until you're heading out the door headfirst. I am never that kind of trouble.

When I enter a place like this—it doesn't have to be the Caribbean Club; it can be a bar in Nebraska or Michigan—I can read the bar like a favorite short story. I'm home, in a sense. Although I grew up in Western Pennsylvania, I don't have the Pittsburghese accent that many people fight to overcome their whole lives. My brother Jeff shows his Western Pennsylvania roots through some distinct Pittsburghese and a pickup truck. Most people guess I come from somewhere vaguely northeast. But my roots show here, at the bar's pool table. Body language and working-class etiquette let my Rustbelt slip show.

Here are the rules (there really aren't any rules): Do not order wine. Do not order a margarita that involves a blender. Do not order any kind of cocktail that would be served "up." Do not talk loudly about academia or feminist theory or your vegan ethics. Do not flirt with the patrons unless you really, really mean to flirt. Do not expect table service. Ask politely when you ask for change for the pool table or pinball machine. If you really, truly suck at darts, do not play darts. Same for pool. This isn't your time. Order something hard on the rocks, or a beer. A simple beer. Do not ask for a fancy craft thing that is locally brewed down the street unless you happen to see a sign for said beer hanging on the wall. Even if you see a sign for said beer, do not start a fancy beer discussion. If you know sports, go for it. If you know basic cooking, cool. Gardening, give it a shot. Almost everyone knows someone who grows tomatoes or makes good sauce. Do not immediately put an hour of music on the jukebox. You may lose all your money and have to sit in silence after the bartender pulls the plug because what you've put on is stuff no one ever plays, and who put that shit on there anyway? Wait to hear what is currently playing on the jukebox and then comingle your tastes with the bar. Put only enough cash on the bar for a few rounds. Leave it there. The bartender will take money out as you drink. Do not put the money back into your wallet each time.

Here in South Florida there are baseball caps and NASCAR posters, T-shirts and jeans, flip flops and tank tops. Cutoffs. Ponytails on men and women. Tough skin. Too much sun. Squint lines around the eyes. The only food served that isn't in a potato chip bag is smoked fish and crackers. The fish comes in a little ziplock bag. You eat it with your fingers. Don't complain.

It doesn't matter where I am. It doesn't matter if I really didn't want to go to the bar in the first place. When I walk in, I'm home. And sometimes across the bar I hear Pittsburghese, because a lot of us ended up in Florida, but that's another story.

According to their website, the Caribbean Club is a place where "locals and tourists mingle." My husband Rick and I have traveled to the Keys to visit our friends Chuck Kinder and Diane Cecily for five winters running. We stay for a month and then head back to finish out the gray slush of Pittsburgh winter. One night when I'm feeling down and Rick is trying to cheer me up, he says, "Let's check out the open mike at this place." The minute we walk in, the architecture of the space puts me at ease. This isn't the crisp white linen fruity cocktail yacht/sailing set. I know—at a glance—these are my people. Or, they are the people I am from.

Not everyone knows how to navigate a bar. By that I mean not everyone is aware of and able to adjust themselves according to the setting. When I walk into the Caribbean Club, I head straight to the bar without hesitation, not a table. I order a Jack Daniels and soda water with a lime. (I check first to see if there are limes and lemons sliced and waiting in little bowls on the bar or I wouldn't ask for a lime.) I don't really drink this drink in my daily life. I'm an Argentinian red wine or Manhattan-drinking martini person these days. I make my own shrubs and tonics. I buy expensive vermouth and bitters. But my drink used to be Jack and soda. Actually it used to be Jack on the rocks, but that's a time I won't revisit as easily. These days I have no problem saying that I'm a writer when asked. I'm a professor. I'm an editor. I don't need Clark Kent anymore, but I miss him.

The man behind the bar is quiet and steady. Rick joins me and orders beer with a whiskey back. One of the reasons I married him is that he, too, can read a space and react accordingly. We met in Lincoln, Nebraska, in a fiction writing workshop. Rick bartended at a local bar, O'Rourke's Tavern. Before Lincoln he worked as a longshoreman in Seattle while writing plays. Before that, he lived out of his van in Colorado. Before that he was one of six brothers sleeping in triple double bunkbeds in his boyhood bedroom in Omaha, Nebraska.

It's early. The pool table is empty. I don't play pool at an occupied table these days. I'm too rusty, and a sucky pool player is no fun. But I am essentially good at pool. I'm good at pinball, ping pong, darts, bocce, skee-ball, and any other kind of recreational sport of this level or one that involves playing cards.

Rick asks if I want to play pool. I normally say no. But tonight I'm feeling blue and I want to reconnect with something.

I say, "Yes. Sure. I do."

He's surprised. "Really?"

"Yes," I say. "Let's play pool."

Rick gets the quarters and hands them to me. I take four, leave the rest of the stack on the bar by my stuff. I love the moment after you fit the quarters into the slots and push and pull the tough metal lever in and out. You can hear the balls roll and rumble into the slot at the end of the table. I love arranging the balls into the black plastic rack, stripe-solid-stripe, eight ball at the center. Pushing them in snug with my knuckles, easing the rack away to leave a triangle of colorful balls shining under the overhead light, ready for the crack of the break.

I'm easing into it, what Rick calls "Beaver Falls Sherrie."

I feel it, too, of course. There's a confidence that surges into my body like a shock, a cockiness. I know this. I know how to operate here. Rick asks me if I want to break, and I say sure. Rick is good at pool. At one point his nickname was Rick the Stick. He's better than me, but we're well-matched, and it was another reason I married him twenty years ago. I needed someone who was both a book-centered intellectual and who could fix things with his hands. I needed to be with someone who knew how to operate in this kind of venue, where the rules are different from, say, a gallery opening, and if you don't care to learn them, you can offend people who don't need offending.

I break. It's a sucky break. I chalk my cue. I'm out of practice. I don't want to be out of practice, but I am. The thing about pool is that it's a public event whether you want it to be or not. The table is lit like a little stage, and you become part of the scene the second you begin, part of the story of the bar that day. We're both a little wobbly but decent enough to keep the game going, and no one else in the bar wants to play. We play another round of eight ball. I can feel the bartender beginning to see me. I suspect he can tell that I belong here, but maybe I'm making that up. I cock my hip. I shoot long, hard shots. My favorites. I hand Rick my empty whiskey glass and say, "Another."

Liz and I sporadically stay in touch in the years after grad school, a phone call here and there. Eventually we connect via Facebook. That's where I see the post. Liz died of breast cancer in May. It seems impossible, but I imagine her feisty spirit staying with her until the end.

I imagine her stomping her way to the other side in her black Doc Martens to wherever we go when it's all said and done. I remember her wearing her red bikini top to class with her bright red lipstick, her straight black hair. She plunks her travel mug of iced coffee down on the table, ready to make an argument, her dark brown eyes on fire beneath her arched brows. She wanted to set a few things straight. And on the surface, those few things encompassed winning arguments about literature. Underneath it all she wanted to be taken seriously.

She wanted to be powerful.

Now I'm left here with hindsight and tact. I'm still just as angry, but I don't wear it on my sleeve anymore. Middle age has given me a new superpower: invisibility. My gray hair, simple tank top, cotton skirt, and Birkenstock sandals are my cape, and they cloak me like Wonder Woman's airplane. There's power in the quiet attack, I've learned. It takes patience to ground and outsmart forces rising to bring you down.

The bar fills. The regulars stream in, and the couple that runs the open mike starts setting up. I feel a moment of reluctance. We'll have to give up the table to better players. But then two college boys on winter break saunter up in their baseball caps. They ask if we're done, and I ask if they want to play, surprising myself and probably them. They say sure. They assume we will suck. I can tell this by the way they begin, ignoring us, continuing their own conversation filled with inside jokes. Beating us will just be a quick, inconvenient blip before they get on with their night. This frustrates me. But this is exactly what I need to get back into my old form. Maybe I'm tapping into something that lives in me that has to do with the dead steel town I grew up in, that has to do with an old anger about being an underdog that can rekindle like a firecracker on the spot. This growing confidence also becomes my feminism coming home to roost.

Power struggles, dominance/submission, gaslighting, sexism. It all plays out right here on this table. Always has. The cock in my hip is my dialect. The sharp bank shot is me calling out their gendered assumptions. Now I'm at home, mad, and just a little drunk. This is the perfect scenario for me to play my best pool. The change is silent—completely internal. My body language shifts again.

And we beat them. And then they want to play again, maybe because they weren't taking us seriously the first time, and suddenly we're holding the table.

I switch to beer, something I never drink anymore. Miller High Life. I'm in the zone. The zone that my upbringing and my schooling and my lived life have brought me to, have taught me to own. From their stools, the regulars, who I don't know, are watching and not watching our little performance. The bartender is doing the same thing. And when we go through the second set of interlopers and I drive in three balls in a row that are ridiculous long shots followed by the eight ball, there's a little cheer from my people at the bar. I look up and nod. Smile, quick and slight. The boys walk away. Another couple walks up and slips four quarters into the slots. I look at Rick and he rubs my shoulder with one hand. I exhale something old and essential. I inhale it again and it fills me up.

This performance is a kind of language. It's a physical dialect absorbed from my hometown that I don't speak very often these days. It helped me through some big changes in my life and became a way for me to transcend the static of academia. It's good to know it's there waiting to remind me of where I'm from and how I came to understand and operate in this feminist arena as practice for what's outside, beyond the bar's door.

CALLING ME OUT

When I moved to Lincoln, Nebraska, in the summer of 1994, it's safe to say I had no idea what I was getting myself into. I had been living in San Francisco's Lower Haight for two years and hadn't really traveled from the Bay Area in the last year at all. It's not that I assumed everyone could buy organic tofu and fresh beet-carrot-ginger juice at the corner market—but I kind of did.

In Nebraska, I reasoned, I would meet cowboys and eat grilled cheese sandwiches. I would score amazing thrift-store deals. It would be an experience. I moved there not knowing a soul. I had never fully dwelled in the conservative nature of the middle. I hadn't deeply considered the overarching, passed-over reality of the Great Plains. This was before Facebook or email, before cell phones and Google. It would be two years before I had my first dial-up connection. I sent postcards to my friends on the coasts, and it took a long time to get one in return. I faced how alone the middle could feel. I felt empathy for the pioneers. Lincoln had a great health food store, galleries, Thai and Indian restaurants, and a film series at the Sheldon Museum of Art. I wasn't so much *culturally* isolated as *geographically* isolated.

Relocating to Lincoln was, as one West Coast friend suggested at the time, "like deciding to move to Mars." Back in San Francisco, at Sally's Bakery, some of my fellow bakers consistently confused

Alaska and Nebraska—saying things like, "Maybe you'll get to see a polar bear?"

"No, Nebraska, the one in the middle? It's landlocked and kind of rectangular with a little knob on the left-hand side?" I would patiently reply.

And they'd say, "Tell me again why you're going there?"

There were other alienating details. My previous jobs had mostly been connected to food—baked goods in particular—first in New Hampshire and then in California. This relocation signaled the first time I had to define myself solely as a fiction writer, the first time I couldn't cling to flour and yeast for an easy definition. I had to step forward with words, and I found this identity difficult to slip on.

Then somewhere along the way, I met Billy Sherman, an artist and photographer who worked as a chef and a contractor in Lincoln. He lived outside of academia, although not outside of intellectual conversation, where I had lived before I started graduate school. Our banter was immediately mixed with food and action—something I was used to. Billy helped tether me to something I recognized from my recent past life.

We became friends in the way that two single people in their late twenties who are sick of relationships become friends. Fast friends who make phone calls in the middle of the night, who meet for breakfast with mussed hair; friends who drive to the farmer's market at 6:00 a.m. to buy sunflower sprouts or, alternately, drink until 6:00 a.m. talking about messed up shit. Good friends.

The first time I went to the Tam O' Shanter—a nondescript hunch of a bar/restaurant on the far end of O Street with a curved red roof and newspaper boxes to the left of the front door—it was in the middle of the afternoon. A blazing Nebraskan summer day, when the sun scorches through your eyeballs to touch the tips of your toes. Take-your-breath-away-you-think-you-understand-hot-after-working-as-a-baker heat.

It was boiling, and Billy had called and left a message on my apartment's answering machine to meet him there for lunch.

The interior of the Tam O' Shanter was dim. 1970s dim. And because of that, cool in a variety of ways. The walls had a fine sheen of red shag carpet, and the curved pleather booths by the bar snuggled people in and made regular old conversations seem important and mysterious. The imitation crystal chandeliers glittering in the corners gave off a subtle, ineffective shine, while cushy black Naugahyde barstools lined up with slender wooden legs in front of the main bar. A "Warm Nuts" machine rested on its counter—salted cashews, almonds, and peanuts gathered in tidy trays, heated by an overhead bulb. There was a slippery quality to the air—dark and moist. Entering the Tam O' Shanter felt like traveling underground. The overlarge door handles at the entrance made it seem part medieval castle, part mafia den. The pebble-pressed concrete exterior did not give away the interior's secrets. You couldn't possibly know the Tam O' Shanter unless you'd been inside, stepped through the red door with the tiny sign that read, "entrance." They served crisp, perfectly fried foods and offered a tiny steak dinner called the Tami. The no-nonsense bartenders made stiff drinks, served in a wide array of appropriately sized glasses. The entire mystique of the place made you want to simultaneously eat french fries, drink a martini, and confess your secret sins.

The first day I met Billy at the Tam O' Shanter was the first and last time I sat in the dining area off to the right of the hostess station. I pushed through the heavy front door, through the vestibule door, and then blinked and squinted my way to him, already seated by the shuttered windows. Billy with his dark wavy hair and black-framed glasses. Billy with his wrinkled white button-down shirt, sleeves rolled to his elbows, with his pursed lips, quick to smile as I told a story. Workers surrounded us, people who did things—measurable things like pounding in nails, like driving trucks. A small TV blinked the day's news in the corner.

Academia intimidated me. I'd spent my childhood in a small industrial, turning post-industrial, steel town. People worked shifts, and
they worked—labored—hard each day with their bodies. They did
this until they were laid off, and then they turned to drinking and
complaining with the same physical intensity at corner bars and
local diners.

My father wasn't a millworker. He was a life insurance salesman and
financial advisor. We lived in a nice house, in a nice neighborhood—
located on a hill above the tiny, gritty city. I descended with my pals to
eat D&G pizza and drink coffee at Eat'n Park restaurant, the Rustbelt
and my father's work ethic seeping into my bones.

Our high school encouraged us to become engineers or pursue
degrees in business. It was maniacal, this push. And so I came to
believe work meant labor—with numbers and formulas and the body
pushing things around. Work meant touching things, not pondering.
And perhaps this was why baking appealed to me, why I applied for
a counter position in a French bakery once I started college on the
East Coast. Soon thereafter I took a job as one of two bread bakers
at another bakery in the same town. Waking up at midnight to begin
a shift, rolling out loaves of oatmeal molasses and anadama bread.
It seemed like the right way to work my way through an English
literature degree.

And yet, there I was, five years after receiving my BA, applying
to graduate school, and then suddenly in graduate school with my
department paying my way. I felt like a sham, a pretend intellectual.
I baked baguettes for my fiction workshop. Cooked elaborate dinners
for myself and Billy. Taught the women writers in my department
how to properly bank a pool ball. Wrote an explosion of short stories
trying to capture the space and sounds of this new place.

The place of Nebraska—its expanse—caused a slow hysteria to build
in me. The sky never ended, and it seemed that one day it would just
up and swallow me if I wasn't careful. The mournful sound of trains

hooting their horns, reaching out over hundreds of miles, broke my heart. The constant wind followed after me as I walked cautiously in my cowboy boots. I nestled my black-framed glasses securely on the bridge of my nose. I searched for bodies of water. I hesitated. I hesitated. I peeked at this flat world, thought it might do me in.

One of the keys to Tam O' Shanter's siren pull was its lack of judgment. It just stood steady in itself while patrons, who did not gawk or pose, came to eat there. They slid into the curved booths wearing their unironic western snap shirts. They walked past the shag-carpeted walls on their way to the bathrooms with pink neon signs above each door announcing "ladies" and "men." I rarely heard anyone whisper, "This is so cool." But it was.

That day, Billy and I hunched over our food, talking about movies, books, art, the failed catastrophe of a date from the previous weekend who *would not stop calling*. We talked with our hands moving, forks swinging, the outside world cut off entirely behind the thick shutters that kept the long rectangle of a room from both sunlight and heat. I felt suspended in time, and this timelessness felt like a cloak of invisibility descending, like a gentle mist of the Prozac everyone in the English department seemed to be taking at the time. *A person could get lost in here*, I remember thinking. Billy was there across from me, smiling his warm, curious smile, digging into a steak, chewing through our discussion, stabbing his knife at the air to make a point. "You are ridiculous," he said. "There is no way you said that to him." We seemed alone in that crowded room. Alone with ourselves, and in this moment it let me take a breath.

The servers and bartenders wore black pants and white button-up shirts. This prim contrast to its bland concrete exterior added to the Tam O' Shanter's otherworldliness. "It was a bar with blue-collar food and country club service," my husband Rick said when I recently asked him to describe the Tam. True. We disagree, however, about where we traditionally sat. I say, in the booth across from the bar where we could be by ourselves but still talk with the bartenders. He says, at the bar itself, on the corner stools under the brass overhang of the glass rack where we sat and talked to the bartenders. And the truth is, we're both probably right. We spent a lot of nights hiding out there. When I first met Rick, not only did Billy approve of him but Rick also already knew about the Tam O' Shanter. Not in an oh-that's-so-retro-and-hip kind of way, but more like—yes, that's the perfect place to drink some whiskey and talk. Let's go.

There was an authentic-ness to Rick that the hipster guys I had dated for years lacked. Rick didn't have a gigantic record collection back at his apartment, and he didn't sport sideburns. His first present to me was a newly purchased bread knife, because he noticed I needed one.

Rick, like the Tam O' Shanter, is from Nebraska. He had grown up in the flat world that was bothering me so much. His slow, one-fingered nod of a hello while driving showed that. He had an earnest, unforced curiosity and said "sack" instead of "bag" at the grocery store. Perhaps in some way, finding this bar led me to him. I'll never know, but it definitely had a part in our courtship, such a big part that we sent a wedding announcement to them when we decided to tie the knot. It hung on the speckled backbar mirror for some time, to the left of the hulking metal cash register.

I had spent my formative years floating in the wake of Reagonomics, embracing an alternative Gen-X worldview where "selling out" was the biggest mistake one could make. Bands sold out when they signed with a major label. A person could sell out by taking a job with a 401K or by turning from thrift-store scores to buying new at J.Crew. I was of this generation that had, instead of dealing with mainstream culture and an administration's priorities we couldn't understand, gone underground for our music and our zines and our humor and our jobs. I dropped out, got into my car, and drove from one coast to another—took time off to explore the crazy mix of small-town and big-city worlds that made up America.

Like my peers, I carefully honed my cool restaurant and motel-finding skills; I had a practiced competitive eye for sifting through a rack to find excellent, super-cheap vintage dresses, sweaters, and housewares. Those cowboy boots that I mentioned earlier that I rarely took off in those days were snatched up in a resale shop in the Castro.

The coasts were, for lack of a better term, competitive in their living skills. Coming to Nebraska let the air out of something I once held dear. In Lincoln I would clutch a trio of vintage La Creuset pans to my chest and scurry to the thrift-store's register like a football player breaking tackles. But no one was really fighting me for the pots. My score was personal. I wanted the pans, yes, but buying them gained me no clout. In this way Nebraska taught me to take a step back, to slow down, take my time, let go.

If I had discovered the Tam O' Shanter on a side street in San Francisco in 1995, I would have immediately sworn to secrecy the select few friends I told about it in order to try and keep its luscious, untouched, eccentric 1970s throwback purity to myself. Located at Twenty-Fifth and O Street, the Tam squared itself off in the corner of a crowded parking lot, near—what was at the time—the less appealing section of Lincoln where I lived, away from the shops, college bars, and the university scene. It wasn't close to the brewpub or restaurants where many of my fellow graduate students and professors gossiped and talked shop. It was, as we liked to say then in our theory classes, "other."

I settled myself in my seat that afternoon, the air shushing out of its black cushion as I thumbed the paper place mat, the cloth napkin. Billy had ordered a Tami. I ordered a grilled cheese and steak fries.

When my sandwich came, the stiff planks of white bread were buttered and golden, a thin line of orange cheese melting out the sides. We each had a beer, and when we shoved open the glass door to reenter the world, it was startling to me that daylight still existed.

The Tam O' Shanter sign had a tiny pom-pommed hat poised atop the cursive *T*, a single right-facing quotation mark following the *O*. It tip-topped a pole that made a stark right angle to the flat Nebraskan horizon. The sign's subtitle read in cursive, "Restaurant and Pub," two generic golf clubs crossed in the empty space to the right. No golf course in sight. Who knows how the place got its name, but it didn't call out for anyone to join in or sell out, just to stop by after work when you had a chance. No pretensions. No looking over your shoulder to see who else was in the bar, to see if anyone from the English department was around. No whispering. No theory. No judgment.

Here I drank my first Rusty Nail, Drambuie and Scotch in a tiny rocks glass, sitting on a cushioned stool at the bar with Rick. Even still when I order that drink I think of flat, heat-blanched lands. I think of fields and their ocean-like rustling, calling me out on myself, letting me let myself back in.

TALK RIGHT

Starting in 1953, my parents Don and Shirley Flick traveled back to their hometown of Tionesta in rural northwestern Pennsylvania every weekend for the first fourteen years of their marriage, picking up eggs from my Uncle Ralph and selling them in Pittsburgh in the early years to afford the gas money to drive back again. Once they no longer needed the extra cash, they drove the four-hour round trip, eggless, to and fro. Every. Weekend.

It took some time for them to uproot. It didn't happen right away in Pittsburgh in the first three years, or Koppel the next six, or in the mill town they moved to and stayed in: Beaver Falls. They engaged with the community, my mother involved in Outlook, my dad in Rotary. They joined bowling leagues. They both volunteered for the Salvation Army and were active in their church and the local medical center board and auxiliary. In fact the gift shop and café at the Heritage Valley Beaver Health System is now named after my mom: the Shirley Flick Gift Shop and Coffee Shop, to honor her long-time service as president of the auxiliary there.

They were civically, religiously, and professionally engaged, but not embedded in the gritty, unionized, linguistic heart and soul of the mill town that America recognizes and knows from popular culture.

Growing up, if one of us said the word "yinz" inside our house, my mom said, "Talk right."

Those weekly trips to the McWilliams Dairy Farm ended in 1969 when I was two years old and Grandma Viola McWilliams died. My brother Dan, twelve years older than I, was grounded and groomed in that rural weekend world of hunting and fishing and riding around on tractors, yet he didn't pick up the yinzer accent that I also do not have.

Dan leans pinball-playing math nerd, and if he ever had visions of joining the mill laborers, they were dashed the summer between his junior and senior years of high school when he worked on an assembly line at the Ward bus company. "If there was ever a motivation to never work in a facility like that again," he told me, "that was it. Steady three to eleven, constant metal filings burning your skin, and hot." Although all of Dan's friends' parents worked in one of the mills in some capacity, many held managerial positions, and nearly all his friends took the academic track in high school and went on to college. Dan majored in math at Carnegie Mellon University.

My brother Jeff, on the other hand, the middle child—a child of the '60s and '70s—absorbed yinzer culture and dialect like a sponge.

Jeff is seven years older than I, and he—at sixty—is still the (now proud) owner of a Pittsburghese accent, an accent that has followed him throughout his professional life. As he told me, he worked for twenty-five years to get rid of it and then gave up.

Jeff grew up in Beaver Falls in the same two houses that I did. He participated in all the classic childhood Americana activities—little league, Cub Scouts, Sunday school, and pick-up basketball with friends. He hit middle and high school during a prosperous time for the mills. B&W (Babcock & Wilcox), J&L (Jones & Laughlin), Crucible, and Moltrup employed over 60 percent of the people in Beavers Falls. The mill workers were unionized and powerful. Whether they knew it or not at the time, that was their heyday.

This day in September 2017, Jeff has just moved into a downtown Pittsburgh apartment in the sleek River Vue high-rise complex on Liberty Avenue. It's the start of a new urban life for him as a divorced middle-aged professional. As an adult he lived in Beaver Falls, raising his three boys with his wife in a big house along Darlington Road just a few houses from our childhood home. He commuted an hour or more into the city to work for thirty-four years. Now his drive is five minutes. A revelation to him.

The 51C bus, which I pick up at Mission and Eighteenth after walking down the Sterling Street city steps from my Pittsburgh home in the South Side Slopes, traverses through the center of the bustling South Side Flats on East Carson Street, crosses the Smithfield Street Bridge with a pretty river view, and then heads into downtown.

The shiny, looming skyscrapers mix with classic architecture and make me look up as I follow the walking directions on my phone. At Jeff's building I can see the Point's fountain spouting in the distance. The place itself is sixteen stories and looms above the intersection, a broad plank of shiny glass and steel.

His apartment on the twelfth floor is tidy—just like his desk at work. And sparse. He brought very little with him into this new life. He has classic rock playing over his living room speakers and a "Big Sur Woods" scented candle lit on the eat-in kitchen table.

Dressed in a black polo shirt and chinos, his salt and pepper hair short and groomed, Jeff is fit and ready for anything I'm about to throw his way. We perch on stools around his kitchen table with tumblers of whiskey at our elbows as the sun sets across the city.

"I had no idea I had any accent until first semester freshman year of college at Bethany," he says. "I had a very heavy Pittsburgh accent with a Beaver Falls dialect and these hillbilly Tionesta-type sayings that everybody said at our house." He laughs. "I come back, and we're having Thanksgiving, and I realize this is where it all came from. Like these sayings, 'Do you want some more mashed potatoes or what?'"

It's true. There are all kinds of sayings like this. Jeff heard them for what they were that day. Hearing them, really, for the first time. That my brother ended up leaving Beaver Falls and attending a liberal arts school in West Virginia is another story in and of itself. Being an unacademic C and D student in high school, he wasn't exactly an in-the-running poster child for higher education. But he was a good soccer player. A fantastic soccer player in a region where, in the 1970s, absolutely no one played soccer. Jeff joined the soccer club at Blackhawk High School. And he worked hard. The soccer coach from Bethany College, John Cunningham, recruited him. But.

"I went down there to play soccer with the idea I'm going to be the starting center forward," he says, "and literally within the first two hours of practice, I'm trying to make the travel team." This is the moment, as he tells it, that he realized he needed to start studying. "All of a sudden I was at this [liberal arts] school. I had great professors. I got here. And now I'm getting this great education. So I go to college, and my first semester I got a 3.96." He slaps the table. "You know what the first thing mom said was? First thing mom said? 'Did you cheat?'" (This comes out pronounced "Djew-cheet?")

"My four years at Bethany, I reveled in that whole thing," Jeff admits. "Every shirt had the sleeves cut off, and you'd have these guys wearing—I used to call them alligator shirts because I didn't even know what they were. Izods. These guys back then, that was the whole preppy thing, they would have two polo shirts with the collars turned up. It was like: I didn't own a polo shirt."

Jeff claimed Beaver Falls pride. His accent, his type of dress—all of it announced our particular brand of Western Pennsylvania. His linguistic claim to mill town came, however, not from our family but most likely from his peer group in high school. As Barbara Johnstone and Scott Kiesling discuss in an essay for PBS' *Do You Speak American* series, "Children learn their accent primarily from their peers, not their parents, and each new group of immigrants to the area learned

English from people who were already speaking English. Dialects spread when people pick up features of the speech of people they are like, talk to a lot, and/or identify with . . ." Jeff's friends, with the exception of one—Denise "Doc" Damazo, whose parents were both doctors—came from working-class millworker households. "Yeah," Jeff says. "Other than Damazo, everybody else, their parents didn't go to college. Everybody worked in the mill. There were many of my friends who were Hungarian or Italian. Either their parents or grandparents came from these countries, and now they lived in the area. I had no friends that I can think of that moved in, like somebody who lived somewhere else and moved into Beaver Falls. I can't think of a single friend, girlfriend. I can't think of anyone that I hung with that wasn't from Beaver Falls, whose family wasn't from Beaver Falls."

Jeff was in and out of these friends' houses where Pittsburghese or languages other than English were spoken. He was on the inside of the mill culture all through his adolescence, surrounded by people who were not trying to break out of it but wanted to continue thriving in it. These weren't friends who prioritized going to college. It was the height of the steel boom, and, as Jeff put it, "You walked out [of high school], you graduated, went down, and got a job."

What you needed to be successful in these jobs was, of course, a strong body, great hand-eye coordination, grunt and pull, and the ability and desire to fit in and work with and against the steaming, sparking industrial elements.

He seems a bit wistful as he continues, "Literally when I graduated high school, it was at the peak of Beaver County steel. And it was in Pittsburgh too. 1978. If Cunningham wouldn't have called me, there would have been a chance, and I don't know if Mom and Dad would have ever allowed me, that I wouldn't have gone to college. I had a lot of friends that went straight to the mill. And they were pulling down—like, in the day, as an eighteen-year-old kid—big money. In my four years while I was at college, it went from the peak of the peak [of steel production], at least in Beaver County, to bust. When I graduated from college it was 25 percent unemployment. So all those people," Jeff says, pausing. "It just changed dramatically in those four years."

According to an October 6, 1982, *New York Times* article, Beaver County's unemployment was at 20.4% the year Jeff graduated. Allegheny County, where Pittsburgh is located, was at 10.7%. Today it's nearly impossible to explain to newcomers to the region what these jarring statistics meant to the present and future of Western Pennsylvania. It didn't help that layoffs in mill culture had been par for the course. Workers would get laid off and then wait to be hired back. It was a cycle. A dance between management and labor. This time the waiting was without end, and many workers weren't mentally prepared for it. Many waited at the bar, short fuses lit.

It's a lucky accident that my brother naively believed he could become a professional soccer player and instead got an excellent education and realized he could instead be an extremely successful, smart, sporty, professional guy.

Around the same time that my brother was making his way through middle and high school, securing his lifelong accent, writer Roy Blount Jr. spent a year embedded with the Pittsburgh Steelers football team. His book *About Three Bricks Shy of a Load: A Highly Irregular Lowdown on the Year the Pittsburgh Steelers Were Super but Missed the Bowl* was published in 1974. In chapter three he tries to explain "Why Pittsburgh"—much of the answer being the local character he had already experienced on and off the field while reporting for *Sports Illustrated*. "I know Pittsburgh, by reputation," he writes, "as a town full of locally famous eccentrics, past and present . . ." Even today this idea of locally famous is taken to heart. I was given, just last December, a shirt that reads "Pittsburgh Famous." A shirt I wear only to garden.

Blount Jr. was enamored with the way Pittsburghers not just talked but also their philosophy on living. "People—including a good many in Pittsburgh—tend to look upon Pittsburgh as a Loser town. Perhaps it is the 'Pitts' in the name, suggesting depression. Perhaps it is the immigrant millworker image of the population. Perhaps it is the fact that Pittsburgh has never been westerly enough to imply frontiersmen, easterly enough to imply sophisticates, or middle enough to imply stolid prosperity." This identity crisis continues even today as outsiders try to place Pittsburgh in the Midwest, which is highly inaccurate if you've ever lived in the Midwest—too much grit. But Pittsburgh also doesn't have enough bravado or pretension to be "northeastern." Really, the West Virginian transplant to Pittsburgh, writer Chuck Kinder, nailed it when he arguably christened the Iron City "The Paris of Appalachia."

Throughout the rest of the "Why Pittsburgh" chapter, Blount Jr. tries to capture the city's particular dialect and chronicle the local color. The accent that he notes, not yet named Pittsburghese, at least not in his rendering here, sounded like this: "'That's all people otta ton think of the Burgh as,' a local bartender told me, 'Soot.'" Blount Jr. continues, "Burghers sometimes refer to their town as 'the Burgh.'" This is still true today. He sounds it out like this: "For the 'ow' sound in words they say something which I have tried to render here with a short *o*, as in 'donton longe,' but which is more precisely, to take the case of 'town' a blend of 'tehn,' 'tahn,' and 'tan.'"

Blount echoes my brother Jeff's experience when he notes that most people he met in Pittsburgh were from Pittsburgh or a town nearby. "There is a dug-in, inveterate quality to life in Pittsburgh. . . . You don't have to drink too many shots and beers . . . in a Pittsburgh bar before you begin to feel the frustrations perking all around you." Blount Jr. calls these frustrations a manifestation of "raffishness." He believed, in 1973, that Pittsburgh was old-school and behind-the-times, that the city had "classic grievances" and "characters in the old sense."

In this same year, out in the bigger United States, Roe v. Wade became law, and the "battle of the sexes" tennis match between Billie

Jean King and Bobby Riggs played out as a manifestation of a growing women's rights movement on a tennis court. The proto-punk
band the New York Dolls released their debut album, *New York Dolls*.
The U.S. involvement in the Vietnam War ended with the Paris
Peace Accords; the Watergate scandal erupted; Nixon resigned, and
the American Psychiatric Association removed homosexuality from
its *Diagnostic and Statistical Manual of Mental Disorders*. At the Art
Institute of Chicago, Andy Warhol, Pittsburgh's then-estranged son,
exhibited a fourteen-foot silkscreen of Mao Zedong in drag makeup.

I wonder how much the accent itself influenced Blount Jr.'s perception of the people he observed. "I never heard the word 'Jagov' so
often in my life as I heard it in Pittsburgh," he writes. "There was an
iron imperative not to be accounted a Jagov. . . . If a lady wouldn't
talk to [a guy] in a bar a Pittsburgher might well walk off grum-
bling, with a hint of desperation, 'I'm a Jagov, right?'" In this chapter
the Pittsburgh identity crisis is contrasted against the controversial yet culturally uplifting catch by the Steelers' Franco Harris: the
Immaculate Reception of 1972 (what Blount calls "the Miraculous
Reception").

I should note, Blount gets the term jagoff completely wrong. First
he spells it Jagov, as if it has some kind of Russian derivation, and he
explains—again incorrectly—that it means jerk-off—like masturba-
tion. Incorrect. The word, spelled jagoff, derives from the Scots-Irish
term for a thorny plant, a jagger bush. Jaggy—sticky—colloquially
means prickly, annoying. A Jagoff, seen today in Pittsburgh, inscribed
on mugs, printed on T-shirts, and emblazoned on bumper stickers
and greeting cards is still something you don't want to be called. It
kind of means asshole, but with a Western Pennsylvania slant to it.

My brother does a good job of disguising his accent in his daily professional life, business meetings, and phone calls. But there are certain
words he can't get right. "There are times for me," he says, "it's hard

even when I'm purposefully thinking about saying something correct that I can't say it. My whole bit is 'keller.' [He means he can't say the word color—this is his downfall.] I think it's how I actually pronounce it: 'Keller.'" He pauses and then tries to say it right, "Coowler." But really, it still isn't right. He sounds like he's trying to say the word color instead of just saying "color."

"It's such a big part of my job [He presents graphic design branding concepts and logos to boards of directors. The word color comes up a lot.], making these presentations so that even just trying to say it—I know what it's supposed to sound like. I just can't. I can't say it." I notice as he talks that when he says "can't" it really sounds like "key-ant." He has no idea he also says that word strangely. He continues, "Dahntahn. Now I'm living 'dahntahn,' but I can say down. Town." He can sort of say it. "I'm to the point, kind of, like when I turned fifty, you know," he says, "that's who I am. Either it's endearing or they think I'm an idiot. I tried to get rid of it. This is the best I can polish it up."

I've heard him compensate for his dialect during business hours by speaking slower, overly enunciating words, and not using contractions. Today, during our conversation, he isn't doing any of that. He told me about a recent big-deal campaign he had to present to a college in Detroit. Part of the strategy was they were going to "Double Down on Downtown Detroit." This is like a joke of a nightmare sentence for someone with a Pittsburghese accent. "I practiced and practiced, and it was like—the third big point. I'm rolling. This presentation is going great, and I literally had practiced this: Double Down on Downtown Detroit. You know where this is going," he says. "And I'm just rolling. And I say it. It was like a minefield waiting to step into. Doubledahn on Dahntahn Detroit."

Jeff drives a pick-up truck, and the valets at River Vue have told him he is the only person in the building who drives a truck. Everyone else drives a fancy car. Jeff loves this about himself. "Professionally, I'm an insider," he says. "I'm connected and know on a first-name basis most of the executives and major players in Pittsburgh. Outside of business, I'm really not. I belong to the Duquesne Club. I go there for lunch and to work out in the gym. I have never really hung in the inside with my age group, with the high rollers. It's not something I aspire to do."

Yet the Duquesne Club is an elite private club downtown. It was founded in 1873. All of the brand-name robber barons spent time there: Frick, Mellon, Carnegie, Heinz, and Westinghouse, for instance. A person must be nominated and then pay a hefty initiation fee and annual dues. Until 1980 all of those nominated were men, as women were not permitted, and still even after they were officially legitimate, only three were initially accepted, and those three still did not have access to the tap room, gym, grill, or *front door*. The first Black people were admitted in 1983. Plans for Pittsburgh's first Renaissance happened here, and I'm sure many other meetings manifesting civic and corporate change in the city. So when my brother says he's not an insider, it's complicated.

He stops for a few seconds and says, regarding this insider/outsider question, "You know, that's a very good question. I've never thought about this before. It's important to me. There's no desire to just do stuff just to be in the [*Pittsburgh Post-Gazette's* high society] *SEEN* column." He pauses again. "I've always been very comfortable being Jeff Flick."

And so, Jeff Flick, at age sixty, has found an equilibrium and a way to pass through the worlds he lives in while operating on both sides of the mill town identity he can't (nor wants to) escape.

Me? I've never had a regional accent, my yinzer comes out as an attitude, not in language. Maybe it circles back to that raffishness that Blount Jr. witnessed in the '70s. It's something my husband calls Beaver Falls Sherrie. When I feel it coming on, I'm either about to really effectively tell someone off, hip cocked, finger pointed, or I'm about to beat them at eight ball at a quarter table in a bar.

By the time I graduated from high school in 1985, the mills were dead, dead, dead. My high school friends and I were college-bound, some out of necessity, and most focused on science and engineering. I was a feminist new wave music intellectual and former cheerleader escaping to the University of New Hampshire to become a writer. I somehow landed back in Pittsburgh again over a decade later, accent-less still, but with the ability to fluently interpret Pittsburghese for my non-native, Nebraskan husband. More than I can count, clerks across the city have asked me where I'm from. And I've said, "Here. I'm from here. I live on the South Side Slopes." And they say, "Yeah, but before that?"

FINDING HOME

The city steps climb the hills. They're stitches that span a history of the place where I live. Workers thumped up and down them for shifts in the mills—thick boots, strong arms, stiff, buckled lunchboxes swinging at their sides. But that Pittsburgh is gone. It echoes behind New Pittsburgh these days, where bike lanes sprout up overnight like dandelions.

I'm laced in up here on the South Side Slopes, settled into an unlikely neighborhood, perched as it is on narrow streets with a lot of impossible access and unlikely houses that have pretty views out over downtown and Oakland. The views used to be of smoke billowing from the factories along the river below, but now they're the kind of homes people in other cities pay real money to live in to see the vistas from their decks and kitchen windows.

How I came to be here, to live in this rusty part of the country, which I'd left decades before, materializes as a big blank screen in my writer's brain. *Why am I here why am I here why am I here* the pigeons coo back at me from the power lines outside my kitchen window. People used to ask me that: Why are you there? But they don't anymore, because now Pittsburgh is new and emitting urban pheromones across the nation. But a city this old and battered can't ever really rise above its roots. So I'm here. Up in the least likely place I could find, surrounded by steps, and surely they're a metaphor for something.

"They often connect precarious and incongruous little spaces with a wormhole's sense of disjunction," architectural historian Charles Rosenblum tells me. "You could be lost on a highway berm, but there's a handrail in an overgrown hillside that will lead you up steps to a backyard barbecue at an above-ground pool."

One day after panting up a steep three-story set of city steps I'd never before walked in my neighborhood, I looked up to find a basketball court: two hoops, the tiniest park, settled into a flat segment of slope. It reminded me of the tennis court I played on when I lived in San Francisco—an equally hilly world. I lived in the Lower Haight, and my boyfriend and I would traipse up some narrow city steps to a single public tennis court with a view. With our thrift-store racquets and not-quite-fresh tennis balls, we had a secret hobby for a while.

So they're an escape hatch. I step up and up and I'm out of the city fray. It feels like the country in the city up here, and the country is where my people come from.

Farms and dirt roads line dusty branches on both sides of my family tree.

It's 1953. Don Flick graduates from Tionesta High School and begins work for the Pennsylvania Highway Department survey corps. When his half-aptly named supervisor Dick Angel throws Howard Raybuck from West Hickory up against a bus and says that he'll beat the shit out of him if he makes a mistake again, my dad knows he already needs a new job.

Ollie Klice hires my six-year-old dad to be his full-time assistant for two dollars a week, carting milk, driving tractors and trucks, and butchering pigs and calves. It's 1941, and my dad lives with his mom, dad, and five siblings in a farmhouse on the Klice Brothers Dairy farm in Allegany, New York. He attends a one-room schoolhouse that has a two-hole outhouse and no running water. Ollie tells my dad he has to do everything at least once on the farm, which includes shooting a pig in the head, dunking it in scalding water, and scraping its hair off.

Ollie nicknames my little dad Popeye after the one-eyed, spinach-eating sailor comic strip and cartoon character. It's 1941, and the United States has just entered World War II. Unlike many other cartoon characters who remain civilians on the screen, Popeye joins the U.S. Navy, dons a white uniform and cap, and serves on a battle-ship. Propaganda reels like "You're a Sap, Mr. Jap," featured Popeye fighting wildly caricatured, racially stereotyped Japanese sailors on screen before Paramount Pictures films in movie theaters of the time. Popeye and his antics would have been on people's minds as men in small and large communities across the nation are drafted to fight the fascists abroad.

I assume my dad is nicknamed Popeye because he's small and mighty, not because he eats spinach or fights bad guys.

He climbs into the cab of the farm truck, pushes the clutch, starts the motor, puts it in gear, then jumps up on the seat to steer. When Ollie yells stop, he jumps down to disengage the clutch again.

Because Popeye is Ollie's sidekick, Ollie takes him to the bar. It's a sober Popeye behind the wheel as they make their way home. When he turns down the lane to the dairy farm, all Ollie's wife sees is a car coming with no visible driver.

You can follow the meandering Allegheny River ninety-five miles south from Allegany, New York, to Tionesta, Pennsylvania. Two hours northeast of Pittsburgh, Tionesta perches at the southwest-ern edge of the Allegheny National Forest in Forest County, one of the least populated counties in the state. It's filled with small farm-steads surrounded by land that was clear-cut and logged but is now a beautiful hardwood forest. There's a rodeo and a strong 4-H presence. Country lanes zigzag through it all. The town sits on the outer edge of Appalachia and proudly flaunts hillbilly tropes that play out in karaoke themes and Halloween costume contests. The town itself has a single commercial street, and there are a lot of hunting and fishing spots.

Tall cornstalks serve as sentries as you drive on the rural routes and lanes nearby. Hay bales spun into giant capsized spools of thread shine in the fall sun. Cows, goats, and chickens chew and run and squawk along farmyards as hunting dogs hold forth on top of their doghouses. A barn cat slinks down a gravel lane, tail tall, hips saunter-ing, a field mouse dangling from its mouth. McWilliams Dairy Farm comes into view after rocking down that long, thin lane for a while.

His sophomore year of high school, my teen dad and his family move to Tionesta, where his mom, Ruth (née Siegworth) Flick, has farm-ing roots. My dad meets my mom, Shirley McWilliams. He plays on the basketball team, and my mom is a cheerleader at Tionesta High, with a graduating class of eight. They fall in love and are engaged at their senior prom.

After witnessing the fiasco with Howard Raybuck, and on a tip from his friend Karl Karlson, my teen dad makes the hundred-plus-mile drive from Tionesta to Pittsburgh, with the Allegheny River guid-ing him south again. He walks into the Westinghouse plant on Penn Avenue and asks for any job that will allow him to take night classes. The personnel manager, Loan Roan, hires him as a core winder. He starts the next week at $156 a month.

My eighteen-year-old parents are soon married and renting their first apartment in Wilkinsburg, a borough adjacent to Pittsburgh's

Regent Square neighborhood, along with my dad's twin sister, Doris, two hours from their families and the rural life they've known.

Both Doris and my mom work as secretaries at Rockwell Manufacturing, and they all split the fifty-dollar-a-month rent three ways. "We ate lots of Spam, potatoes, and things we could bring back from the farm," Dad tells me.

My mom would say here that she made more money than my dad when they got those first jobs. And she swore that after she got married she would never hold dinner for anyone like her mom had done for the farming men. Those realities would change, but both parents tell me they didn't miss living in Tionesta—the clear skies, the fresh air, the rural life. My parents settle into the crowded, smoky, sooty city with coal-burning stoves and steel mills churning twenty-four seven.

Every weekend my parents drive back to Tionesta to eat supper at the McWilliams' farmhouse on Friday and Saturday, and then on Sunday they eat lunch at the Flicks'. Both the Flicks and McWilliams have large clans—six in the Flick family and thirteen in the McWilliams.

My mom plays cards with her sisters—Edna, Lois, and Arlene. My dad hunts and trout fishes with my mom's brothers Ralph, Harry, Russ, Ken, Gene, Harley (called Jake), and Maurice (pronounced Morse). My mom's sisters, Arlene and Lois, make the same weekly weekend trek from Erie with their husbands and children in tow. They all check in at the McWilliams' farm upon arrival, walking through the farmhouse's slamming screen door into a long bustling kitchen.

The farmhouse itself isn't strung to electricity until 1945. At this time, the cooking is still done on a hulking hybrid gas and wood, mint-green-and-tan enameled cookstove. Everyone eats, often in three shifts, women and girls last, down a long table in the dining room with leaves from the table stretched over chairs to create extra seating along the windows. A small gas heating stove with ceramic tiles thumps and hisses on one end of the room in the chilly months. Sticky fly strips hang along the periphery when it's warm and the windows are open. A slight stink of manure pervades the home from the dairy barn up the hill. It's a pleasant mix of manure and milk—it haunts the corners. "I don't know how Grandma and Grandpa McWilliams put up with us," my dad says, "but they'd be upset if we didn't come home."

My mom sits across from me in a booth at Eat'n Park in downtown Beaver Falls, where she and my dad moved when they were twenty-six. Salty roasted peanuts perch atop our matching Tin Roof sundaes, under a little tent of whipped cream topped with a cherry. It's 1998, and I've just moved to Pittsburgh, back to Western Pennsylvania, after having bolted in 1985 when I graduated from high school. I've wandered all around, temping and baking and eventually going to grad school. I'm called a free spirit in my family. I've been directed to call home weekly, on Sunday nights, collect if I need to, and haven't.

My mother asks if Rick and I will be coming to supper every Sunday now. I feel like I have to squint to see her way over there, waiting for my answer.

By 1955 my dad's salary is up to $250 a month, my brother Dan is born, and they move into a bigger apartment. "Somewhere in the process, our Pittsburgh friends knew we were going to the farm in Tionesta every weekend," my dad says. "I told them Shirley's brother had a chicken farm." At first my dad carries a few dozen eggs back for friends, but then the word gets out, and he soon has *customers*. Since my parents have some difficulty affording the twenty-five-cents-a-gallon gas they need for the weekly round trips, my dad decides to charge people ten cents more than he pays for the eggs, and the Egg Route is born.

When my husband Rick and I move into our first house on the South Side Slopes of Pittsburgh in 1999 there are very few windows that face the pretty view in our neighborhood. Just smooth, straight backsides stare out over the Monongahela River. The expanse below had once been many homeowners' place of employment, J&L Steel, spewing smoke, hulking, glowing on the horizon. Something for a house to turn its back on, really, focusing on the life lived inside, on everyday comings and goings.

One day Rick gets out his Sawzall and cuts a big rectangle into the plaster in the living room. He kicks it out and steps onto the back porch roof, surveying our Pittsburgh kingdom, hands on his hips, laughing. The neighbors look up at him from their tiny backyards.

The window seat we build beneath the big picture window looks out over Oakland and Downtown Pittsburgh. Barges move lethargically on the river, puffy trees and storybook houses dot the hills, the Cathedral of Learning dominates Oakland on the other side of the river, while downtown skyscrapers jaggedly announce the blue sky like exclamation points on the western horizon, where J&L Steel once smoked and brooded over many city blocks. Bulldozers are moving around piles of dirt like a giant sandbox, and there are plans for a shopping center and apartments. The mill's Hot Metal Bridge, which once carried crucibles of molten iron to the open hearth furnaces on the opposite bank of the Monongahela, will become a pedestrian and bike path eight years later. The other half, which was once a railroad bridge, will carry cars across the next year.

"Stairs were a later addition to early houses," Rosenblum says. "The first added levels were attics accessed by ladders. Stairs take up valuable space and funds, so, as with anything in architecture, a larger and more elaborate one is a means to flaunt wealth." The houses on the Slopes aren't flaunting much, and their staircases, albeit on the inside, are narrow and steep with uneven treads. When we walk the stairs down to the kitchen in our new home, it feels like we're entering the hull of a boat. Everything has a homemade air to it as we start in on renovations. Floors aren't flat; walls aren't straight; the hearth we expose is poured concrete with marbles halfway pressed into it by a previous creative and frugal inhabitant.

We pull up the shag carpet, pull down the fake wood paneling, and dismantle the drop ceilings. When we gut the horsehair plaster from the living room, releasing decades of coal dust and soot, we also expose charred beams that aren't all charred on the same side. A thrifty builder must have salvaged them from a burned-down house somewhere nearby when building this one.

The sweet old woman we buy the house from stops in one day while visiting friends on the street. She knocks on the doorframe and pokes her head in to see me standing ankle-deep in rubble in her former living room, a crowbar dangling from one hand. She says, "What in the fuck are you doing?"

My dad picks up the eggs in Tionesta each weekend and then delivers them at the plant in Pittsburgh on Monday morning before his workday begins. "Management, security officers, secretaries, people from all parts of the plant were my customers," he says. By this time Westinghouse has moved into a four-story building in East Liberty, radically upping potential egg sales. The egg route explodes to over a hundred dozen per week.

There's my young, optimistic father walking into the vibrant plant, into stark industrial rooms with his flat-top haircut and black-framed glasses, with his wool plaid shirt and peg-leg pants. Wires buzz with electronic progress, as he carries in trays of freshly laid eggs.

Ralph, my mom's oldest brother, a gentleman farmer, keeps the chicken coop at his place just over the hill from the dairy farm. He gathers the eggs each day and carts them to the springhouse and through an egg washer. The second level of the springhouse is damp from the creek running through the room below. It smells of chicken feed and grains and is cluttered with egg baskets and binder twine. Ralph makes batches of dandelion wine each year and stores it in the springhouse to keep it cool. "He would offer me a drink from time to time," my dad says. "It was real smooth."

My dad rigs a candling device, checking each egg for the blood spots that his fussy urban customers don't like. The double-yolk eggs, on the other hand, are extremely popular. At the peak of his egg business, he has to visit three to four other farms to fill his orders. From December 1954 to June 1957 my brother Danny is wedged into the car along with the eggs, suitcases, and the bags of canned goods and garden produce Grandma Flick hands out.

Grandma Flick cultivates a huge, beautiful hillside vegetable garden that the Allegheny, which runs along the bank below their house in Tionesta, floods most years. She's an obsessive canner, pickler, quilter, and rug hooker. I remember the taste of her unsweetened Concord grape juice and her sweet-and-sour pickle relish, always served in a cut-class bowl. She kept a tin of homemade sugar cookies on the kitchen counter, and her basement shelves were lined with a wide array of home-canned fruits, vegetables, and venison that she would load into a basket, shoulder to shoulder, and hand out with a nervous laugh, folding her empty hands in front of her, already anxious to start on another project.

The Leticoe Steps make up a rickety paper street that turns into a real street, directly across Barry from Stella, the first street we live on in the South Side Slopes. A tread is missing midway, and the bottom wooden board has a wonky rock to it, so walking down these stairs takes some finesse. As I ease myself down, I descend like an escalator past some tiny front and side yards and then step onto Kosciusko Way en route to my first job in Pittsburgh at a pottery studio on the

Flats. Along the descent there are a series of openings in the railings that lead to walkways to the homes that line the steps. A stout man with a Liberace haircut, who wears a fancy, knee-length, zipper-front embroidered women's housecoat in electric blue with pointy, ornate slippers on his bare, manly feet, sweeps his walkway. He chats amiably down to a fellow neighbor puttering on his truck's engine on the street below.

My dad inches up another rung in the tall Westinghouse ladder to a position working directly with the engineers. They're pleased he's taking night classes, and they help him with his homework when he has spare time. Most of my dad's fellow employees at Westinghouse are from the Pittsburgh area, so a boy who migrated in from the country is a novelty to them.

"They seemed to be very interested in Tionesta," my father says. So he invites them up to stay in a hunting and fishing cabin there—a camp. My dad is good at identifying the commodity of "the country" and packaging it up. I remember him still doing this kind of thing to my high school and then college friends. Wanting to show them how cows are milked or driving around with a flashlight on country roads "spotting" deer at night.

My dad's coworkers let loose when my dad takes them away from the city. Post-college boys on a jaunt. "Their actions were out of this world," he says. "So much noise and a lot of kidding." They drink and carouse at the local bars, maybe feeling more anonymous than they could in the city. My straight-laced and underaged father does not. "I did not," he says. "I stayed at the cabin."

I imagine him building an orderly fire, settling sticks and then logs onto the crackling flames. He's pacing himself for success, knowing it's a fragile path. A young guy with no connections and no money for full-time college. He's all by himself near the rustling woods, waiting for the whooping drunken city men to return.

In July 1957 my dad leaves Westinghouse and his pursuit of a college degree. He and my mom decide to move to Koppel and then Beaver Falls, Pennsylvania, where my dad trains to become a life insurance salesman so he can make more money right away. This is the career he dedicates himself to for the rest of his life and the end of their urban life. The end of one possible timeline, which is reset and redirected, and then on course for the next six decades.

The Egg Route ends, and my dad's customers return to buying regular, boring eggs at their local supermarket.

When my parents settle there, Beaver Falls is a thriving industrial mill town with an enviable shopping district. The town curves along the Beaver River about forty-five minutes north of Pittsburgh. My dad needs a map to find it the first time because everything up that way is uncharted territory for him.

For my parents, the decision to move away from their home and families was rooted in the practicalities of advancement and success based on getting ahead, moving up the financial ladder. Of course, they weren't alone in pursuing fiscal success mixed with white-collar mobility, in moving away from the farm and to a desk job. The United States was changing, and they were a part of it all. My parents had high, idealistic hopes, in keeping with the pursuit of the American dream. My dad believed, simply, if he worked hard he could succeed. It was one of the most appropriate American decades for a young, white couple to chase it down.

They still live in Beaver Falls today, but they purchased Uncle Ralph's farmhouse in 1987. It's now a weekend retreat for my family, and where I got married twenty-three years ago. The chicken coop is gone, although you can trace the outline of its stone foundation. The springhouse remains the water source for the farmhouse. When my parents bought the farm there were still a few jugs of dandelion wine in there. My dad was tempted, but he dumped them out.

As I walk the Mission Street steps they're straight and lean. From the bottom to the top it looks like Bubby, my Yorkie, and I will climb right into the clouds. In fact, in historic photos many city step landings look like diving boards out into a vast, awaiting city.

We clunk, clunk, clunk on the hollow concrete stairs past fenced-in barking dogs, up toward the blue sky. And then up again at the Oakley Street steps where we meet another dog walker—we bark and nod to each other respectively.

Here on the Slopes, my dog learns "up" and "down," along with "sit" and "stay." And Bubby is pretty fit.

It's quiet, and we're the only ones on the stairs after the dog walker descends toward the Flats. It used to bustle up here. Tiny houses packed with big families, workers on three different shifts clomping up and down these steps.

In a black-and-white photograph from 1930 that I find in the University of Pittsburgh digital archives, a tall corner store rises at the base of the steps where I'm standing right now. Every Day Milk, Mother's Quick Oats, and Heinz pickles are displayed through its plate glass window, which boasts Salada Tea in simple arched lettering. A metal sign tacked onto its wooden clapboard front poetically declares: Eat / Denver / Sandwich / Candy 5 Cents.

Now it's nothing. Air.

The sizzle of commerce isn't here anymore. There are a few tiny bars left and a restaurant in a former union hall, UUBU 6, a restaurant that started up with big hopes and good reviews in 2006 is now, although still sporadically open, perpetually for sale.

When we first moved to the Slopes in 1999 several houses on our street had just sold for $6,000, and Mission Street Market, with its famous home-cured deli sausage a couple blocks away, was still open.

I walked there each Sunday to buy a *Pittsburgh Post-Gazette* and a paczki donut made on the Flats by Greb's Bakery. The market delivered and kept running accounts for the older folks in the Slopes. When I walked through its doors, it felt like traveling back in time. This world I now lived in was a stark contrast to where I'd lived previously. The city felt dead. We had moved there to try and resuscitate it a bit. Rick recruited some investors who bought a seven-story building downtown for a song and converted it into artist studio space. We waited around for things to start happening.

The Mission Market would close in the next few years because the owner's sons weren't interested in keeping the business going. Today it sits empty with dusty paper covering its windows, some drooping because the tape has long since lost its stickiness.

In 1999 our first home cost $28,000, and I thought we paid too much for it. Up and down the curving streets and hills, houses stood in homage to the 1980s—shag carpet, wood paneling, and drop ceilings inside, aluminum siding and big hulking awnings on the outside. What worker would invest in cosmetic renovations after layoffs, after the mills shut down? Pittsburgh was a city frozen in time.

Bubby and I walk past a bright green piano on the sidewalk and many No Parking signs. A Pittsburgh Pirates flag snaps in the breeze. A gray cat—suspicious of us as I search in vain for a set of steps that should lead us back but have seemingly disappeared—tucks his head down and squints from under a car. We wander around in the sharp morning air. Later we retrace our steps the way we came as the dog chorus blooms again.

I knew the second we drove into these steep hills that I wanted to live in the South Side Slopes. The beautiful light. The views. The quaint, crumbling, nonsensical infrastructure. The many, many sets of city steps zipping it all together. It charmed me and reminded me of places I'd previously lived. But these houses were *cheap*. We didn't really consider the logistics of day-to-day existence or resale values. We didn't consider jobs or futures. Instead we went with the romantic notion of being tucked into these fairytale hills in a tiny house that really was the stuff of fables.

These days, we take walks in the newly refurbished, fifty-seven-acre South Side Park. To get there we walk up Eleanor and then the Sterling Street steps. If we stop at the entrance to the park, where a recent No Hunting sign was just installed, and look up the hillside to the left, we often see chickens strutting in their run. A couple of dogs bark at us from balconies built with a view to the city. My friend Tracy tells me that pre-COVID-19, the guy with the chickens was selling his eggs. We walk on the narrow path that leads into the woods where the deer and hawks make nests. We circle through the forest trails and head home.

REBEL, REBEL

Embark on a guided float trip that is wacky and irreverent while paying tribute to the 1790s Whiskey Rebellion. We'll tell the story of this historically significant rebellion in an entirely new way—by hearkening to the voice of David Bowie. Why Bowie? We believe that a spirit of rebellion—revolution even—threaded the experiences of the rebels and David Bowie (albeit nearly two hundred years removed). We'll use music and interpreters in such a way that you won't possibly forget what the Whiskey Rebellion meant to both the region and a young nation.

They also promised two cocktails and a rustic riverfront supper.

A day dedicated to kayaking, David Bowie, and the historic Whiskey Rebellion with actual whiskey available to drink? What could be wrong with this mixology? I sent an email to a small group of people to see who wanted to join me, and two of my writer-editor friends said yes.

This is how I found myself in my driveway on August 6, 2017, with Christine Stroud of Autumn House Press and Beth Kracklauer of *The Wall Street Journal* strapping two kayaks to the roof of my car and looking at my back tire saying, "Doesn't that look a little low?" The strapping of the kayaks on the car is not a task that falls under my domain of required household skills. My husband Rick does that job, and so I was a bit nervous that the two boats would fly off the car as we slanted it downward out of the South Side Slopes of Pittsburgh. Still nervous even after I texted Rick a photo of the strapped kayaks and he wrote back, "Looks good."

The tire just heightened the tension. It looked really low. We loaded up and set out to find some air. The first GetGo's pump was broken, as was the CoGo's pump. The second GetGo I remembered, which was by accident on our route, did the trick. The tire was very low—a slow leak I'd find out the next day—and then it was filled and we were trekking on borrowed time to the town of Monongahela, wherever that was, my GPS leading the way. We had our water bottles and our sunglasses and a vague, useless sense of where we were going as the loose strap ends that we hadn't secured properly onto the lassoed kayaks broke free like victory flags. We traversed PA 43 South to PA 136 East. The straps continued to flap in the breeze as I questioned our route asking (more than once), "Where is the water?" We seemed to be driving through an industrial wasteland. Eventually Christine grabbed one strap after rolling down a window and pinned it inside with us. I tucked in the other.

Even as we neared the drop-off point for the kayaks, we all had a little doubt as to the legitimacy of the event. We rocked over some train tracks, circled around a park, and joined a few other forlorn-looking kayakers who met us with an equally perplexed, "Is this the right spot?"

One of my biggest complaints about Pittsburgh when I first moved there in 1998 was the plethora of non-event events. These were events that looked great in the arts listings and had good descriptions but when you arrived were basically a keg party in a big room. Non-event events are my cultural nemesis. In fact, their proliferated existence prompted me to cofound and run a monthly literary reading series for a decade in Pittsburgh in the early 2000s. The Gist Street Reading

Series, I swear, did not disappoint as an event. Held on the third floor of James Simon's sculpture studio with a bathtub filled with beer, a table of wine, homemade bread and ice cream made by Antoine, James's next-door neighbor. Each month writers from across the country traveled to Pittsburgh and walked up two flights of steep stairs to read poetry and prose to a sold-out crowd.

Today's unlikely program had a lot to pull together after that enticing description.

I had feared a trove of hipsters at the drop-off, but instead there were a bunch of legitimate kayakers there. People who had nice setups and some great storage compartments and good nerdy sun hats. I was encouraged that it was, it seemed, the kayakers and not preening Bowie fans who'd come out.

We registered, pored through a pile of Bowie fake tattoos, and helped ourselves to fresh peaches from a local orchard loaded into a box at the end of the table. We applied our tattoos, took photos of the applied tattoos to post to Instagram, donned our sunglasses, and mingled with the rest of the thirty-five participants. The event was sold out, even after the first scheduled date a week earlier had been canceled due to high water and storms. Everyone seemed authentically excited. The vibe wasn't ironic. It wasn't overtly artisanal or serious. Several people wore Bowie concert T-shirts, and we were all super ready to geek out over him, historic Whiskey Rebellion reenactors, and paddling on a semi-industrial river. With that in mind, the DJ stopped, and one of the historic reenactors—who had until that moment been simply milling about in his eighteenth-century American garb like a regular person from 1794, picked up an acoustic guitar and started playing Bowie's "Rebel Rebel" with a slight twist on the lyrics. It all made sense. Bowie was a rebel, and the people who took on the American government over taxed whiskey were rebels too. Logical!

We had to wonder who the mastermind was behind this brilliant hybrid three-ring-circus of an event. And I soon found out: Amy

Camp. Amy introduced herself to me before the Whiskey Rebellioner started belting out Bowie, and she noted that her wife was doing the awesome job of DJing.

Amy runs a one-person consulting firm called Cycle Forward, and she sometimes, like with this event, works with the Mon River Towns Program, whose goal is to help communities along the Monongahela River recognize the river as an asset and draw people out to use it. Since the Mon played a significant role in the Whiskey Rebellion, that was an easy thematic fit to pair with a Mon River kayak experience, so Amy reached out to some historic reenactors. They decided to give a few perspectives of the rebellion via roving soliloquies.

I met up with Amy a few months after the event on a sunny morning in Wilkinsburg, a borough adjacent to Pittsburgh that has seen enough new growth in recent years to garner its own funky coffee shop. Amy looks younger than her forty years with a bright, sunny face and a big, encouraging smile, just the type of person to convince an organization of the natural connection between an uprising about taxation and a sometimes cross-dressing intergalactic rock star.

"How it happened was so random," she said. "I was letting the program sit for a while because I couldn't come up with a good name, and I was just playing around with the word rebellion, and 'Rebel Rebel' popped into my head. So then I just started to think: Is there anything we can do to connect Bowie's music to the Whiskey Rebellion? And strangely enough we found a way to do that. It was so great that one of the actors played guitar."

Back at the event, the actor portraying the radical Mingo Creek Association whiskey rebel John Holcroft had finished singing "Rebel Rebel," and the actor playing whiskey rebel David Bradford's wife, Elizabeth Bradford, stepped forward to deliver a rousing introduction: "These are a people who do not take injustices lightly, and these songs of this Mr. Bowie, they seem to speak to this very experience," she said clutching her hands together earnestly in her period kerchief and dress. "We will share our stories. You will paddle on the river. And the music of this Mr. Bowie will tie it all together." And with that we life-vested up and got ready to kayak.

The town of Monongahela, seventeen miles south of Pittsburgh, situated in Washington County, was founded in 1769 on the confluence of Pigeon Creek and the Monongahela River. Whiskey Point, a bluff in the city, was an important meeting place for delegates of the rebels to discuss submission to the new governmental tax on whiskey. This, after they'd tarred and feathered a few tax collectors, burned down some houses, threatened to burn the city of Pittsburgh to the ground, and caused enough of a scene to pique the interest of Washington and Hamilton over in Philadelphia—then the capital of our nation—who came to consider them a serious enough threat to the stability of the new democracy that Washington sent thirteen thousand troops over the treacherous mountains to see what was what in Western Pennsylvania.

Important to this story is the fact that around the time of the Whiskey Rebellion there was one whiskey still for every ten families in Washington County. Rye whiskey was a valuable commodity for Western Pennsylvania farmers. Easier to transport than grain that had a finite shelf life, the settlers had a brisk and profitable sales market over the mountains in the east. These Scots-Irish and German pioneers were good at making whiskey. They'd had practice. "They brought along with them a deep knowledge of distilling. In Europe, they'd used malted barley for their whiskey mash, but barley took poorly to the new land, so they used rye, which adapted much quicker," Bryce T. Bauer discusses in his article "The Fall and Rebirth of America's First Great Rye Whiskey: Pennsylvania Rye" in *Punch*. This whiskey was soon a favorite of the settled lands in the east. "As Americans began to give up rum following the Revolutionary War," Bauer continues, "whiskey became the de-facto currency of the western Pennsylvania farmer-distillers' barter-based economy."

In the meantime the government was looking for a way to pay off its war debt because income taxes and property taxes didn't yet exist; they zeroed in on the successful western front rye whiskey as a solution to get out of the red. Tax the whiskey. Easy solution. The rebels saw this as a big guy versus little guy thing. Why should the little guys fund a government that wouldn't even help them establish better trade routes to the West for their whiskey? For the rebels, this whole scenario was a bit too close for comfort to the British taxing their tea—a fight they had just fought and won and were, apparently, willing to fight again.

Back at the Rebel, Rebel event, an actor playing Albert Gallatin, a moderate representative from Fayette County who had tried to reason with his more anarchist-leaning whiskey rebels, tells us, "As we speak, I have word that an army of nearly thirteen thousand men are marching over the mountains to end what those in the East are calling the Western Insurrection. They call us treasonists and say we should be dealt with accordingly. This will be the death of our protest. . . . Most likely the death of most of us. What will your families do if you are not there to care for them? Of what consequence will your death be because of one tax upon them? I do not say that we should not continue to fight this tax, but rather we do it through peaceful means." Gallatin nods. John Holcroft storms off in a radical huff. We push our boats into the water.

The town of Monongahela doesn't feel very historically important. Today, like many small economically depressed towns in the United States, it's part of an ever-increasing opioid crisis. In Washington County there were 109 accidental opioid deaths reported in 2016. According to a June 2017 article in the *Pittsburgh Post-Gazette* there were also more opioid criminal cases than alcohol in the county in that same year. Industry left the region long ago. Or, like at the Clairton Coke Works ten miles up the Mon, the industry spews particulate matter at alarming rates. Recently residents have brought a class action lawsuit against U.S. Steel there. According to an August 2017 *PRI* report Clairton Coke Works violated its air permit 6,700 times between 2012 and 2015. Cancer rates are up. Poverty rates are up all across the Mon Valley. There's a hollowed-out, lost quality to the town of Monongahela itself. You can sense from its main street that it was once bustling but is now a remnant of that once prosperous past along with the other towns that skirt the river south of the city: Homestead, Braddock, West Mifflin, McKeesport, and Clairton. Beth and Christine confirm that they hadn't known the town of Monongahela existed until today.

This day we are a group of predominantly Gen Xers paddling on the murky water nearby after some brief instructions for the novices amongst us from a representative of Venture Outdoors, a Pittsburgh-based organization that provides equipment and instruction to get people into nature. The water is filled with debris from recent storms. Wood, walnuts, plastic bottles, and Styrofoam nestle up to our oars as we move forward en masse, like a raft of ducks, upriver. The tall banks expose sloping backyards that end with some rickety boat docks at the shore, trees, and some suspicious bright brown runoff. Abandoned, enormous hunks of steel machinery loom over us along the banks. It's cool, paddling in this quiet, post-industrial nature, very different from paddling on the rivers in Pittsburgh or on a lake in secluded nature. "It's beautiful," Christine says, "but sad." Western Pennsylvania is steeped in this sad nostalgia. There's a loss that can still be viscerally felt, especially in these towns outside of the city: there was something bigger here once, and the ghost of that abundance still takes up space.

The paddle is about an hour. Midway, our Venture Outdoors leader herds us back. As we round a bend in the river, we see, as a complete surprise, none other than our historic reenactors set up in the distance and playing Bowie's "Young Americans" on the river's bank.

We paddle up, a little stunned at this post-modern historically inaccurate—but thematically apt—impromptu concert on a little piece of land jutting out into the river. A small boy out riding his mini dirt bike on the nearby lane stops to take in the whole scene before his dad saunters over from a pickup truck and guides him on his way again. Elizabeth Bradford is on the tambourine, John Holcroft plays lead guitar, and Albert Gallatin is stroking the washboard. They have a thin, silver music stand propped up in the gravel with a few sheets of music on its ledge as they switch to, again, conceptually on target: "Pressure."

When I asked Amy what theories she had in mind when creating the event, she said she always wants to create programs that engage all the senses—smell, sight, taste, touch, and sound. She wants it all to be there to help bring ideas together. She didn't necessarily see this Whiskey Rebellion/Bowie event as kitschy or tongue-in-cheek. She earnestly wanted participants to think about and make some real connections between these seemingly divergent themes. The water and the whiskey and the peaches and the tattoos and the DJ were all there to make the experience complete.

Rebel, Rebel wasn't Portland cool. It wasn't hip. Instead it had a homemade, sincere quality to it. "I feel like there's no way to say this that doesn't sound corny, but it felt soulful," Beth Kracklauer would later tell me. "It felt like something that if any kind of marketing or PR person had got their hands on it, it would've not happened. It was a thing that was just almost like two people who got a little high and were drinking on some bourbon and were like, 'What if . . . ?'"

Amy notes that they kept trying to figure out who the event would attract. Boomers? Millennials? They hadn't anticipated a whole gaggle of Gen Xers, but demographically that's what happened. And since Gen Xers have grown up in the shadow of two monster generations, we really appreciate it when something accidentally but totally hits the mark with us.

The whole event was refreshing and, it seemed to me, very Western Pennsylvania—when Western Pennsylvania is working at its very best. As we pulled our kayaks ashore we readied to drink cocktails made by Pittsburgh whiskey distillery Wigle Whiskey, which was named—not accidentally—after Whiskey Rebellion rebel Phillip Wigle, who was one of the hardcore, kickass house-burning rebels. Wigle opened to the public in 2012 and is the first rye whiskey distillery to operate in Pittsburgh since Prohibition. Owners Mark Meyer and Meredith Meyer Grelli were in some ways more history nerds than booze aficionados when they first started the business. In 2017 they published *The Whiskey Rebellion and the Rebirth of Rye: A Pittsburgh Story*, a book that outlines the details of the Rebellion and ventures into what it means to be a small rye distillery in Western Pennsylvania today. In her introduction Meredith admits, "We are not a family of barflies. We are a family that loves great food and drink, history, and our region of Western Pennsylvania."

But before we made our way up to the grassy shore where there were picnic blankets stretched out and pot pies made by the Pittsburgh bakery Prohibition Pastries—everything they bake has booze in it, we heard from actor John Neville, the whiskey rebels' nemesis. Neville, a military officer and tax collector, sparked the tensions of the Whiskey Rebellion by actually trying to collect the whiskey tax from Western Pennsylvanians, and he was the only collector in the country to do so. The whiskey still owners of Kentucky, a state founded only two years earlier in 1792, for instance, just ignored the tax altogether. In fact, after this whole rebellion was quelled many of the players sauntered on over to Kentucky to continue avoiding the tax and to discover what it means to make whiskey with corn instead of rye. And this is how Kentucky bourbon was born.

In response to his law-abiding idea of tax collecting, the rebels burned down Neville's house and demanded his resignation, among other things. Neville called on Washington to send troops, which he did, but Washington didn't convict them all of treason in the end, which he probably could have, and that is supposed to make Washington a good guy. He did march some of the rebels over the mountains in brutal conditions, and he did deprive them of food and water, but that's the confusing detailed real history we never learn in school. Now, with his arm outstretched, Neville says, "People of the West . . . Go home. Go home and feel blessed that you do not live under the rule of a tyrant but rather a president who sympathizes with you and is willing to forgive your trespasses." We kayakers had suddenly turned into the band of whiskey rebels. And in some ways we were: we still pay that whiskey tax with every bottle we buy in the United States. Gallatin looks a little forlorn as he plays one last song: Bowie's "Heroes," just before we strap our kayaks back onto our cars and wander uphill for some whiskey, which we deserve.

ALL IN THE FAMILY

WALDO AND HIS GHOSTS

Across the street the pigeons strut along the peak of the pink house's roof. They pace impatiently, jostling each other every so often to get ahead in line. Also every so often they rise up as a group, wings flapping, and then settle their plump bodies on restless little legs again.

At the house to the right of ours, Bert heroically fills her birdfeeders each morning. There are long, skinny feeders for the finches and wider feeders for the squabbling blue jays. The pigeons hang out like it's an all-you-can-eat buffet and they want to get their money's worth. They spread out, pecking the ground, spilling over onto the driveway and road. They seem to eat in shifts away from the pink house—bird workers—but they all end up back over there when they've clocked out, admiring the stunning view of downtown Pittsburgh and the neighborhood of Oakland across the Monongahela River.

Waldo lives in the pink house, the house he grew up in, which is the house his father grew up in and the house I'm pretty sure his great-grandfather built. I'm not sure if it has always been pink, but rumor has it that Mrs. Waldo, his mom, always dressed to the nines. It's a pretty racy color for the South Side Slopes of Pittsburgh. But I imagine some great-grandmother, grandmother, or mother along the way found a good deal on pink siding, and that's how it stands:

a big pink house in a workers' city that pops out from the gaggle of houses on the hills that you see as you drive across the Birmingham Bridge into the South Side of Pittsburgh.

Waldo believes the pigeons that roost on his rooftop are descendants of the homing pigeons his father, Jimmy, raced. Waldo says Jimmy was the pigeon racing champion of Polish Hill, which was what this part of the Slopes was called back in the day; the term Slopes didn't fully crystalize until the late 1990s when the South Side Slopes Neighborhood Association was formed, reinforcing that the hilly part was one neighborhood, distinct from the flat part of the South Side.

There was a coop at the Waldo residence all through Waldo's childhood, but the birds were never pets. His mother would frequently have him fetch a few for dinner. Waldo credited his long life to his childhood diet of pigeon.

Every time a lightbulb blew in the house, Waldo's father ground it up into a powder. For a long time, Waldo didn't know why. That is, until Jimmy was caught putting the crushed lightbulb into his pigeon feed before races. The birds would fly home fast because their guts were cutting up and bleeding, and I guess they just wanted to die at home in their own coop. Jimmy was banned from one club because of this behavior, but according to Waldo, he just joined another one.

There's a long history of betting on stuff in Pittsburgh. Numbers running comes up in August Wilson plays and in most old-timers' stories. It's a type of illegal betting historically popular in poorer, working-class neighborhoods. A "runner" runs betting slips from people's homes to an unofficial betting "parlor." These were bars, clubs, and barbershops. People try to guess numbers that are "called" the next day. Rumor has it that numbers running officially hit Pittsburgh around 1927 when Gus Greenlee, the owner of the Crawford Grill jazz club and the Pittsburgh Crawfords Negro league baseball team, shifted from rum-running to number running. Illegal backroom betting was still very much a thing when I first moved to Pittsburgh in 1998, which was why many people were against building the new, legitimate casino that ended up landing on the North Side.

Horses, dogs, and pigeons were no exception in the betting pools. There were many pigeon racing clubs in the city, and apparently the largest pigeon supplier in the country, Foy's Pigeon Supplies, founded in 1883, is still alive and kicking in my hometown, Beaver Falls. They sell three thousand different pigeon items, including pigeons themselves, which can be shipped one-day air by the USPS.

The pigeons comfort Waldo. Sometimes he sits on his back porch looking out over the city of Pittsburgh, shaking a can of corn just like his dad used to, calling the pigeons home to him. Waldo believes the ghosts of his mother and grandmother still reside in the house. He talks to them every day. For him, the house is alive with family. His one wish is to die at home, alone.

Out at the feeders, the pigeons do their cocky dance amongst the doves and jays, chickadees, finches, and robins. Bert also puts out a tray of peanuts for the squirrels. No one seems to mind the pigeons up on the Slopes. It seems weird that they hang out away from the urban core downtown. I like to imagine they take second and third shift down there later in the day.

The morning Waldo died—and he did die alone in his home—a full kit of pigeons lined up on his roof and all along the maze of power lines running in front of his house and mine. They weren't pacing. They didn't rise and descend. They just sat somberly in a line, wings tucked in, beaks facing forward. Before the ambulance arrived I noted their quantity as I drank my morning coffee and looked out our big kitchen window. I called my husband to ask if he'd heard from Waldo lately.

Now the pink house sits empty, which is still surprising because Waldo had been the center of our daily lives for some time, a constant presence from across the street, the knower of facts and teller of stories, the giver of dog treats, the demander of beer, whiskey, cigarettes, and rides down to the Polish Falcons club.

It's statistically improbable that Waldo lived as long as he did, which was until age eighty-three. He started smoking when he was eight years old. When the doctor told him he had lung cancer, he talk-yelled back at him, "Spots on my lungs? Of course I have spots on my lungs!" But then Waldo just lived and lived and lived, continuing to smoke and drink until nearly the very end.

Not everyone on Holt Street socializes with one another. In general it's a pretty closed-up street. But Waldo socialized nearly every day in the warm months out on the bench in front of his house. At night, Gil from down the street would come over; they'd eat pie and ice cream and watch old westerns and other shows on the flat-screen TV that my husband Rick won in a raffle the day before Waldo's old TV died.

The day we closed on our house on Holt Street, Jim, the neighbor across the street and next door to Waldo, came roaring up in his pickup, which he planted in the middle of our narrow one-way street. When we told Jim we planned to live in the house, not rent it out, he told us we were crazy, that he'd been trying to get out of the Slopes forever. And soon he did. But this day he pulled the gate of his truck down with a clank and, without comment, carted a big, dead deer out, down the steps, and into his backyard, where I assume he hung it up and did the kind of butchering that my family would do in the countryside, where it would seem normal.

I was sorry to see Jim go, but he was replaced by Margaret, who is—for lack of a better term—one of us. A Carnegie Mellon University graduate who works as assistant director at the Miller Institute for Contemporary Art, she creates esoteric sound installation performances around the city with her partner, Michael. Eventually she and Michael became part of the small corps of Waldo caregivers who served as extended family, buying groceries, cutting his grass, and listening to his rambling, advice-giving conversations. This isn't to say that this essay is about gentrification, because the Slopes isn't gentrifying anytime soon. Houses are passed on from one generation to the next for a dollar, and there's a stagnant air that has settled in, which makes most house flippers regret or abandon purchases. The roads are narrow; the houses are falling apart; the world is high up and closed off.

By spring of 2017 we'd been settled into Holt Street for fifteen years. It's around this time that Rick and I purchase sneakers. Mine are bright, multicolored New Balance, and his are vegan Saucony. We get them on sale at DSW. I post a photo of our feet wearing these shoes on Instagram and hashtag it #exercising.

We've decided to start walking the Eleanor Street Steps every morning after we drink our coffee. The world has gone a bit crazy and our solution is to walk until we huff and puff and have to take breaks because these stairs are insanely steep, descending past houses and into the overgrown foliage of knotweed, trees, and trash.

Some days it feels urban-tropical. Some days it rains. Some days it's colder than it should be. We leave our Yorkie, Bubby, behind, much to his dismay. These are head-clearing walks, not dog walks. It's the kind of thing I need in order to think more deeply about stuff, as the view of Pittsburgh's skyline spreads out before us. Our neighborhood is comprised of sixty-eight sets of these public steps, some standing in for roads on maps—called "paper streets," or a street on a (paper) map only, not in reality. Eleanor Street, the part that cars drive on, runs almost the length of the Slopes from bottom to top. It becomes a paper street where it meets Holt and turns into a stairway without warning. Drivers need to turn right or left and let their GPS find a different, more circuitous way to get up or down. It's confusing to everyone except those of us who live here.

We lace on the sneakers, roll up our jeans, put on old T-shirts and flannel shirts and rain jackets, and head out, down, and then up.

I'm about to turn fifty in July, so I'm thinking a lot about exercise, legacy, home, and what that word *home* means to us Gen Xers now that we're middle-aged, of all things.

Some days Rick hums the theme song to *All in the Family* as we walk toward our chosen staircase. It's lodged in his head because on Sunday nights he walks over to Waldo's at 6:00 pm to watch two reruns of the show back-to-back. Waldo, born in 1935, the same year as my father, comes from the Silent Generation just like Archie Bunker, the patriarch of *All in the Family*, played by Carroll O'Connor, and his wife Edith, played by Jean Stapleton. Meathead, or Mike Stivic, the live-in son-in-law, played by Rob Reiner, and Gloria, Archie's daughter, played by Sally Struthers, are Boomers. This show was first broadcast for those two generations, battling it out in 1970s America, beaming into thousands of households as tiny Gen-X children like me sat in living rooms watching too.

I would have been four years old when the show debuted and twelve when it ended. Yet I already knew, as I sat watching TV in my parents' sunroom, wearing little-girl clogs and polyester halter tops, that I was on Meathead's side of the argument—the liberal, hippie, intellectual side—even though the rest of my family was probably in many ways rooting for Archie.

I distinctly remember sitting with some visiting relatives, and because we have company the TV is turned on its wheeled pedestal from the small sunroom into the bigger living room. An episode of *All in the Family* plays, and Archie is talking about gay people. This talk, even though I don't fully understand it, lights up a little alarm in my child brain. Gay is taboo in mainstream American culture of the time, and I don't even know what it means, but know I shouldn't know. I sit very still, electric with alarm, as my father and uncles chuckle.

"Judging Books by Their Covers" first broadcast on February 9, 1971, and is notable because the first gay character in a U.S. sitcom was introduced that night, according to A. J. Aronstein, writing for

Vulture. The episode pivots on the joke that Roger, the flamboyant friend of Mike and Gloria's, who is just back from Europe, isn't the gay guy; it's the sturdy beer-drinking ex-football player Steve. "That big football player is a flower?" Edith asks.

Part of my electric shock in the memory has to do with the fact that these things were not discussed in my home and also because the word "gay" is never used in the show. "Flower" and "fairy" and "fag" and "queer" are used. I'm sure I didn't know what they meant in this context. I'm sure I didn't actually know what gay meant, just that something dangerous and unknown was happening on the TV, but my relatives were chuckling about it—not discussing it, just chuckling. And that's the memory of *All in the Family* that stays with me.

Rick and Waldo watch two episodes back-to-back, and when Rick returns he reports on theme, plot, Waldo's reaction, and how the snacks I've sent over were received. Waldo loves the poppyseed cake but not so much the banana bread with walnuts and crystallized ginger.

Around the time *All in the Family* beamed into American living rooms, *Good Times, Maude, Sanford and Son,* and *The Jeffersons* were on too. They all tackled taboo subjects and were all written by Norman Lear. The thing I find interesting is that the home/apartment rests solidly at the center of each show. If we think about *All in the Family* and the way it critiqued American society in a time of cultural and political turmoil through Carroll O'Connor's character of Archie Bunker, we need to think also about how the house itself in the show demonstrated all that Archie had worked for, how he wanted the world outside his Queens neighborhood to remain the same, just as the knick-knacks remained on his own shelves and his recliner remained in front of the TV beside Edith's armchair. But, of course, with Meathead living under his own roof, we see Archie can't even keep the world *inside* his home from changing.

From 1971 to 1979 *All in the Family* served as a warning sign to a certain segment of the viewing population and an affirmation for another. Each show broadcast the not-so-subtle message: *change is inevitable*. Although set in Queens, Bunker's cookie-cutter house, street, and working-class vibe could have easily been any Western Pennsylvania mill town or Pittsburgh neighborhood, could have been Beaver Falls or the South Side Slopes of Pittsburgh or Waldo's pink house on the hill.

Rick grabs a hard cider from our fridge, changes into clothes that will soon be saturated with cigarette smoke, and walks across the street and down the short set of city stairs to Waldo's place. They've become unlikely friends—a Nebraska-born transplant and a hardcore Pittsburgh native—the two getting closer as Waldo ages and spends more time at home and less time at the Polish Falcons club.

The day Waldo died, Rick wept at our kitchen table.

The beauty of Lear's writing is that Rick and Waldo don't laugh at the same parts. Like a Looney Tunes cartoon that speaks to both children and adults, *All in the Family* appeals to two audiences simultaneously—the progressive and the conservative. As an eighty-two-year-old working-class guy from the Slopes, Waldo is there, right there, with Archie. But Waldo is a smart guy and starts to pay attention to Rick's responses.

Change is happening all around Archie in 1971 and now around us in Pittsburgh and elsewhere in many of America's smaller cities that have been in decline since the late 1980s. Pittsburgh, once the poster child for the busted-out, beaten-down, polluted Rustbelt city, weathered the post-industrial storm and has risen up in recent years to become a media darling: "Built on Steel, Pittsburgh Now Thrives on Culture," *The New York Times*, 2017; "Why the Future Looks Like Pittsburgh," *CityLab*, 2017; "Pittsburgh Shows the Way to a Rust Belt Rebound," *Bloomberg*, 2018; "How Pittsburgh Became America's Most Unlikely Cultural Capital," *The Telegraph*, 2016; "New Meets Old in Pittsburgh," *Chicago Tribune*, 2014; "What Millennials Love About

Pittsburgh," *The Atlantic*, 2014; "What Pittsburgh Can Teach the Rest of the Country about Living Well," *The Huffington Post*, 2013; etc.

Although I'm not Archie Bunker, I'm often disgruntled these days when reporters come to Pittsburgh, stay for a weekend, and do not get my city right at all. Pittsburgh's culture and what it is that draws people in and makes them stay can't just be found on Butler Street in hipster Lawrenceville, in chef-centered restaurants showcasing the local and sustainable, in one visit to Gooski's dive bar, or on a single ride up the Duquesne Incline to Mt. Washington to see the fine, clear view of the three rivers. Pittsburgh has a dormant quality—it resists being easily known. It's a contract you only understand after you've dug into the place for a time. It isn't midwestern; it isn't northeastern. It's the Rustbelt, and in my experience Pittsburgh kind of seeps into you and you into it. After you've lived in it for a time—say twenty years—you get it better, but never *right*.

There's the yell-talking quality to the dialect that gets my heart purring when I hear it in its purest form. I grew up in this region, so it brings me to my roots to hear a couple ladies wearing pastel pedal pushers and white Keds in line at the Giant Eagle grocery store with canned pineapple and Chiclets and marshmallow fluff in their carts and rollers in their hair talk about Tommy and how he's doin' and how the girls are getting big and how the church sale is next weekend and how Rhonda has promised to take them down. It's the combination of the old and new that interests me these days. I feel like the reporters want to subtract the old or just use it for T-shirt slogans and dive into the new. But it's messier than that. And not everything is working, of course. Those two sweet old ladies might be as racist and homophobic as Archie.

The *All in the Family* episode that hits home for Waldo is "Lionel Moves Into the Neighborhood." It originally aired on March 2, 1971. As the episode begins, Archie silently reads the newspaper in his recliner. After Meathead and Gloria show up, he reads aloud,

"Unemployment at seven-year high. Rise of strikes expected here. No end to inflation seen."

"Nixon predicts great year," Meathead replies. The live studio audience laughs.

Soon thereafter Louise Jefferson, who is Black (and Lionel's mom), knocks on the front door. She has come to pick up the key to 708, a house down the street. But Archie thinks she's soliciting and tells her that he gave at the office. Louise also asks to borrow a pail and then Archie assumes she's a maid come to clean the new owners' home. Edith runs to grab a pail and the key, and Archie and Louise stand awkwardly inside the front door. "How'd you like the Julia show?" Archie asks. "How did you like Doris Day?" Louise responds. More in-studio laughter. And with that comparison, the racial contrast is set for the viewing audience of the day. *Julia*, a sitcom featuring Black actor Diahann Carroll as lead, first aired in 1968 and ran until 1971. It was groundbreaking because Julia was a nurse, not a maid or any other Black stereotype. She was a young widow trying to raise a young son. This day, Louise Jefferson is picking up the key to her own home, which she and her husband George have bought in a predominantly white neighborhood.

Three years earlier in the real world outside of TV land, President Johnson signed the Civil Rights Act of 1968, which prohibited discrimination in the sale, rental, and financing of housing. Louise's unexpected presence on Archie's doorstep becomes Lear's exploration of this act in real time.

When we made the startling realization in 1999 that buying a house would be cheaper than renting in Pittsburgh, I was immediately drawn to the Slopes of the South Side. The narrow streets and tiny houses. The excellent views and light. It reminded me simultaneously of two places where I'd previously lived but without the coasts or upward mobility. The houses were so cheap. I assumed many young people like us would join in.

I was wrong about that. Today the Slopes are still pretty much the same as when we moved in. There are more decks and some experimental condo units here and there. Some people have caught on to the views, but really not that many. I feel hidden in plain sight. "It feels special to be a part of this secret," my neighbor Margaret says, "to know my neighbors and the nooks and crannies of the wobbly city steps, to live in this tiny bird's nest high on a hill in Pittsburgh."

As we parked on the crazy narrow streets and ambled up front walks to houses with our suit-wearing, white-Cadillac-driving, gum-snapping real estate agent, neighbors frequently eyed us up from their porches. Many of them said something akin to, "You're white. Thank God. We don't want no Blacks moving in here." They said this with no qualms, to our faces, in broad daylight, in 1999. Sometimes they used the n-word instead of Blacks. They might as well have been Archie Bunker saying, "Let's see how wonderful it is when the watermelon rinds come flying out the window."

And then we would cross that house off our list.

Back in 1971 as the Vietnam War raged and Nixon sat in the White House, the culture wars hit the streets and the airwaves in the United States. "A Republican loading-dock worker living in Queens, Bunker railed from his easy chair against 'coons' and 'hebes,' 'spics' and 'fags.' He yelled at his wife and he screamed at his son-in-law, and even when he was quiet, he was fuming about 'the good old days,'" Emily Nussbaum writes in "The Great Divide: Norman Lear, Archie Bunker, and the Rise of the Bad Fan" for the *New Yorker*. The night the first episode aired, extra operators stood by to field complaints from the viewing audience. They even placed a disclaimer at the front of the show warning it used laughter to examine our "frailties, prejudices, and concerns." No calls came in. By season two the show had blasted expectations and 60 percent of the viewing public watched on Saturday nights—more than fifty million viewers.

The South Side Slopes was and is a predominantly white neighborhood. Polish, German, Ukrainian, Irish, and white Eastern European immigrant workers built the simple houses we now live in and walked down the city steps to work at the mill or in a factory, where they sometimes mingled with Italian Americans and Black workers.

"The hospice nurses, every single one of Waldo's in-home caregivers, were Black," Rick says. "Initially Waldo would laugh at the racist stuff on *All in the Family*. He actually thought it wasn't a good idea for the Jeffersons to come into Archie's neighborhood. But he saw me laughing when he wasn't. And then we started discussing it."

When the hospice workers first started coming to Waldo's house, he was not pleased that they were Black. He called them all kinds of names. But they didn't (or couldn't) go away, and then—in his Waldo way—he got to know them as people.

Millie and Eugene were his two main caregivers. "Millie started bringing her son along to Waldo's," Rick says. "I would guess maybe he was eight when she first started bringing him. We basically watched him grow up. He was just becoming a teenager when Waldo died."

Rick knew Waldo's worldview had changed when Waldo turned in his chair to look him in the eye and said, "You know, I always thought I'd be young a long time and then I'd be old a little while and then I'd die . . . but I've been old a long time." Waldo just went on living and living and living, but because he couldn't ramble around and drink in the South Side bars, he had a lot of time to think.

The day after the 2010 Snowmageddon snowstorm brought Pittsburgh to a standstill and made nearly every road impassable, we walked door-to-door taking orders, and then we hiked down the city steps to the South Side Flats Giant Eagle to get supplies for our neighbors. We didn't yet know Waldo well, but I decided that he shouldn't eat white bread. I don't know why I made this executive decision amid Snowmageddon in the middle of the South Side Giant Eagle, but I insisted we buy soft whole wheat for him, which Rick immediately intuited was a bad idea.

"What the hell's that?" Waldo talk-yelled at me as I stood in his doorway. Rick said, "It's wheat. We thought you should eat wheat. It's better for you."

Waldo talk-yelled back, "I'm not eating that shit."

And then my Beaver Falls kicked in and I talk-yelled, "You should eat it. It's good for you." And Waldo continued to rant that he was only eating his white bread and he didn't eat brown bread and we could go to hell for bringing this other bread home. Even in the middle of a complete-city-shutdown-level snowstorm.

And Rick did, in fact, walk back down to Giant Eagle, through snowdrifts and the icy cold, to get him a new loaf of white bread.

That is when Rick's friendship with Waldo began. "I noticed a week later the wheat bread was there uneaten on the counter," Rick tells me. "He wasn't about to touch it. But he also wasn't going to throw it away. He never threw away food. He'd eat green baloney." After all, Silent Generation babies were the offspring of Depression-era parents. And those frugal ways run deep. I see it in my parents, and I saw it in Waldo's way of working the system until he had free twenty-four-hour in-home caregivers, the way he mail-ordered his cigarillos from a place in New York to get the best deal, and the way he drank the absolute cheapest beer he could find.

Waldo had been a city walker like me. I used to pass him as I made my way down the Sterling Street steps to catch a bus or as I took the circuitous Barry Street steps up to the Slopes. But after Waldo tripped on the icy Leticoe steps, he couldn't get around very well anymore. Before that, he'd owned a car, but his Ford Escort died in front of our house in a prime parking spot and sat there for months until Waldo's son Greg came in from Virginia, called it dead, and had it towed away.

All of Waldo's roving ended after his fall. "It was Valentine's Day, 2011," he tells me. "Cause I left here seven o'clock in the morning, went to Giant Eagle did my shopping, stopped and had some beers, and even Joe on Mission Street told me, he says, 'Don't use the steps; they're icy.' And I said, 'Hell, I walked down them this morning.' I had my snow treads on. I said, 'No problem,' but I had two shopping bags, and I was coming up, and I slipped, and when I slipped I grabbed the rail and went backwards and bumpity-bumpity bump."

He was never the same.

Soon Rick and Margaret and Michael and Joe the ex-marine (not to be confused with Joe from Mission Street or Joe our next-door neighbor) started watching out for him. Rick would regularly go down to the Flats to get Waldo in the football polls at the Polish Falcons club and the White Eagle bar and pick up his winnings. Through Waldo, Rick got a membership to the Polish Falcons club. Ten dollars a year and he could take Waldo there for early afternoon drinks.

Soon after the Snowmageddon bread incident, Rick started picking up Waldo's beer and whiskey, and he'd fix little things in his house—a leaking toilet, a burned-out lightbulb. After he was done with his task, two shots of whiskey would appear on the counter. Rick never saw Waldo pour them, and it didn't matter if it was 9:00 a.m. or midnight. "It was an offense if I didn't drink it," Rick says, laughing. "Waldo never laughed or joked around about it though. Apparently his mother poured a glass of Manischewitz for any worker who came to the house."

Waldo was suspicious of us when we moved into the neighborhood. After all, we were related to no one, Rick hadn't even been born in Western Pennsylvania, and neither of us was Polish in any way. After Rick started diligently drinking his shots, we became part of the fabric of the Slopes, as Waldo defined it.

In "Lionel Moves into the Neighborhood," Archie Bunker's neighbor Bowman says, "I sold to Blacks, Archie, because I am tired of hating people." Bowman says he believes the bumper sticker: "Good neighbors come in all colors." It's clear from the studio audience's response that they don't believe Bowman. He sold his house to the Jeffersons because they offered him decent money for it, and he wouldn't be around the neighborhood for the fallout. Bowman suggests that Archie rally the neighbors to buy the house back in order to "sell to one of our own kind." He says, "They'll be tap dancing back to Harlem."

Back at his own home, Archie tells his family, "Jim Bowman sold his home to a family of spades." Archie worries about the value of his home plummeting. He says, "Our world is coming crumbling down. The coons are coming."

Edith says, "Well, you sure gotta hand it to them. Two years ago they was nothing but servants and janitors. Now they're teachers and doctors and lawyers. They've come a long way on TV."

Edith, in her high-voiced, "dingbat" way, is right, of course. Civil rights advances allowed for some leveling up in fields that hadn't been previously possible in the 1970s. But that didn't mean that roadblocks didn't and still don't exist. Pittsburgh is one of the worst cities in the nation for Black women to live, according to a 2019 study by the City of Pittsburgh Gender Equity Commission. In 2020 Pittsburgh City Council declared racism a public health crisis.

"Waldo was Archie Bunker," Rick says. "The last people to get satire are the people being satirized. He slowly realized that."

The show helped people witness the complexities of their changing world while laughing. "The things people care about the most are the things they laugh hardest at," Norman Lear told Bill Moyers in 2015. "And laughter and tears run hand-in-hand. And it's kind of nice to get people—if they're laughing hard enough, perhaps—to try to move them to tears, but with a basic premise that people will laugh harder if they're caring."

"The show was partly created to help people like Waldo catch up with how fast the world was changing," Rick says, "and it didn't work on him when the show aired—or he didn't watch the show back then.

While we were watching the show, I think Waldo actually became a better human being."

The day the pigeons lined up in droves outside my kitchen window, the ambulance came and then the coroner. Waldo died alone sitting at his kitchen table while Eugene was on his way to his next shift. His death is just a little poof in the scheme of things, but change is change, and Waldo saw the world differently before he left it. He made unlikely friends and started to understand his invisible systems of hate and soften them at the corners. And because he believed he'd stay around in some way after the fact, I like to believe that changed energy remains, floating around over there in the pink house that a flipper bought but now sits empty as yet another contractor has been stymied by the logistics of the South Side Slopes.

These days pigeons still line up on Waldo's roof. I like to think the lone brown bird is Waldo himself over there impatiently checking out the skyline. He has a few choice words for the guy who bought the house before he flies over to Bert's to eat. But for now he looks out at the same expanse that generations of his ancestors have known. And like all the other pigeons, he flies away but always turns back, trying to get home.

CULTIVATION

The real estate agent who shows us the home on Stella Street can't get the key to work in the front door lock. It's a sunny early fall day coming off of loads of gray rain. Rick and I stand around in the sunshine on the quiet street, the windows of the row houses that line the two sides blink at us. *Outsiders*, they say.

The agent calls the owner. This won't be a problem, she assures us, winking. The little old lady arrives in a huff, gets the key to work, and then tells the agent to get it together. We smile, say hi. Smile some more. Step inside under the striped aluminum awning.

The little blue row house sits on the lower level of a bi-level street. The upper level carries people in and around a long curve, parading past all the houses on the loop, and the lower level escorts them out, past the blue house, where you have to park your car on the sidewalk with the passenger side snugged up tight to the house in order for there to be room for other cars to ease by and onto Barry Street.

We walk through the simple rooms at street level. Brown shag carpet, thick, tan drapes, blinds, drop ceilings, and brown paneling, and then down a staircase to the kitchen at ground level. Nubby blue carpet. Through the kitchen and out the screened-in back porch, we step into the tidy grass yard, which reveals a surprisingly open view of Oakland across the river. A view that would mean expensive in a different city, but not here.

The moment I walk out into that view, into the airy yard, I think, GARDEN. I think, I'll learn to compost and save seeds and grow vegetables and flowers. My brain packs itself with this new idea in all caps. It hits me in one giant thrust of nesting. I want this house and this yard, and even though it's the first home we look at, we buy it.

How I ended up in Pittsburgh is a good question to ask at the time. One day I'm thriving in a PhD program in the Great Plains, funded and teaching. The next day, I quit.

It isn't that simple, of course. First Rick and I leave Nebraska for a spring break trip back to my homeland, where I meet up for coffee with my old friend and poet Nancy Krygowski who is in the MFA program at the University of Pittsburgh. While we drink coffee at 61C Cafe, gossiping and mulling over the world, Rick drives around, falling in love with Pittsburgh, its bridges and rivers, old buildings and old-timey bars. Rick starts looking at these crazy cheap warehouse buildings that he thinks would be perfect for artist studio space. It's 1996. I'm about to finish a master's degree in English literature with a creative thesis in fiction. I'm about to enter a PhD program I had zero intention of starting just a couple of years earlier. Academia has its cult-like traits, and when you're good at theory and good at writing there's a lot of *why not* floating around. There's a lot of *just keep going.*

Rick and I marry in the summer of 1997. Rick moves to Pittsburgh to manage a building he found some investors to buy to convert into nonresidential artist studio space. He names it the Warehouse Workshop. On Second Avenue right on the edge of downtown Pittsburgh, it's a seven-story concrete row house warehouse building that used to house the American Thermoplastic Company, founded in 1954. They made three-ring binders and outgrew the building in

1994. Rick begins the work of prepping the spaces and defining the code. He finds a tiny one-bedroom apartment in Squirrel Hill with brown shag carpeting, brown paneling, and drop ceilings.

At the closing table, I talk with the previous owners about tomatoes and cucumbers: Have they ever grown them? The grown son, who is about to place his mother into a nursing home, leans forward, suddenly earnest and interested. He says, "You can grow anything in that soil. Anything except cucumbers."

Back in 1995 I have just met Rick. We're both graduate students at the University of Nebraska. In my second year of the master's program, he's the new guy in the fiction workshop. When Rick wanders into the coffee shop where I've camped out before class and sits down at my table, I wonder what that means. When he visits my apartment for the first time, potted plants line my sunny windowsill, every one near death, turning toward crispy brown.

He says, "Were you away for the summer?"

I say, "No, why?"

"Your plants, they're dead," he says.

"I know," I say. "It's just too much work. You know, keeping them green?"

We marry and then Rick lives in Pittsburgh and I live in Nebraska, the way so many couples swing it in academia. No problem. It's fine, except I don't want to be a professor, live on the Great Plains, or be apart from my husband, and I'm not keen on the priest they've allowed into a graduate-level writing workshop who is interested in saving my soul based on the content of my short stories.

I wake up one morning a year and a half into the PhD. I blink in the expansive Great Plains light that streams through the lace curtains in my bedroom windows. I hear my landlord, who lives downstairs, turn up some old-time music, the kind he plays on his excellent weekly radio show. My cat Nicki sits on my chest and meows. I say quietly, *I quit.* Once it's said, out loud to myself, I can't seem to take it back. It's so obvious that I fit in and I don't fit in, that I'm an intellectual's intellectual and I'm also not. I'm just. I'm funded, I'm fellowshipped, and I'm just. Done. I want to be a writer, but this isn't the way. So I resign.

I throw a goodbye party and then leave in a U-Haul on Christmas day December 1997, driving with Rick to Pittsburgh, a Christmas bulb hanging from our rearview mirror, my long-time road trip car in tow behind us.

Everything is fine except for the gigantic depression that descends like wet wool across my body. I suddenly no longer know who I am or what I'm doing, and I've just free-floated back to where it all began. It's a depression that slams me horizontally to the couch in our brown apartment with my white cat and a husband I adore who now works twenty-four seven to make a building for artists who maybe don't yet even want studio space in this city. It rains and snows through Pittsburgh gray skies every day for the first three months of 1998. I sink further into the couch cushions.

I eventually get up off the couch long enough to get a part-time job at a pottery studio, then a job at the Frick Art & Historical Center where I am resuscitated amongst a department of badass women into a museum education curator for the next seven years. I'm a mill town escapee, returned to the region of the crime, working at a robber baron's estate. The complexities are not lost on me.

I'm not a prime candidate to become a gardener. I've spent years leaving. Relationships, places, apartments, jobs. An easy equation: get into the car and drive. Sunglasses reflecting the horizon, an arm out the window, red lipstick, cut-offs, a T-shirt. Turn the key and go. My girlfriends and I have a motto through the '90s: if you're not having fun, leave. And even though we don't always act on it, the idea guides us away from many boundaries that want to fence us in.

I know that leaving can't be forever, that even the open road can get stale. I know I have to figure out a way to *stay*. Stay in a marriage, stay in a place. Root. Find myself again.

When we move to Stella Street two widowers bracket us: John and John. John on the lefthand side ambles out to his tiny second-floor porch with his black dog Midnight and sits each evening, silently watching the sun set over Downtown Pittsburgh. This view would have been a somewhat new revelation in a neighborhood that previously overlooked thumping, pumping, sooty steel mills.

He eventually ambles back inside, and that is that. We faintly hear his cane tap through our shared wall.

Eventually, though, John talks to me about tomatoes. From his second-floor perch he leans toward me standing in our tiny yard and explains in his still-thick Polish accent that he only eats fresh tomatoes in the summer and store-bought canned tomatoes in the offseason. He reminds me to pick off the sucker leaves on my plants, to not plant everything so close together.

I haven't considered when I should and should not eat a tomato. I'm just learning what it means to grow food. John no longer has a vegetable garden himself, but he has stacks of garden tools tucked into the rafters below his back porch. A wide band of bright red tulips outlines his yard along his chain-link fence.

John only talks to me, never to Rick, even if Rick stands right beside me. I walk into my yard, and his eyes light up, and he says, *Sherrie*, and we talk gardens, even though I have no idea what I'm doing.

Each morning from his porch he throws bread out for the birds, mostly crows. After eating their carbs, the crows pull my pepper seedlings up from the ground I've just cultivated.

John on the righthand side serves defiantly in his role as the elderly patriarch widower, ordering around his grown daughters when they visit and sternly sitting in a stiff lawn chair, scowling at the view. He admits he made a mistake by building a fence short of his own property line, so a little swath of our lawn is his. He says it's okay to plant my beans in it anyway. He softens a bit after the garden is in full swing, tells me I plant everything too early and too close together, but my lettuce looks good.

A day or two before he dies, right after he has come home from the hospital after a heart attack, he's out mowing his lawn with a manual push mower. "I can't believe I can't get this done," he says, red-faced and panting.

The coroner comes to the house with his hearse snaking the top and bottom of our street. He drives the body away.

After lefthand side John's health starts to fail, his good son moves him into a nursing home, and his other son scrambles to shove, push, and pull all the family antiques out of the house in the dead of night. We walk past him awkwardly shuffling a tall dresser out the door and into his truck, but we don't really understand the yin and yang of what's unfolding until we talk to the good son days later. In his final act of defiance the other son yanks up all the blooming tulips, roots and all. I witness the shocking slaughtered flowers the next bright Pittsburgh morning as I step into my garden, a red-petaled, bloody mess across John's yard.

I eventually jump the chain-link fence to pluck some from their hostile death. It feels like I'm messing with someone else's metaphor, but I stick them in my little garden where they continue to bloom the rest of the springs we live there, which aren't many.

The good son is left with an empty house and downed tulips. He stands in the backyard, hands in his pockets, quietly explaining that his brother is a very angry man. The good son sells the little house to a large extended family, which eventually forces us out of our own house and up the hill to Holt Street, but that's another story that involves miscommunication, large stereo speakers placed against a shared wall, screaming, bad logic, an above ground swimming pool set up on a sloped yard—filled and drained more than twice—and one family member sitting on the second-floor porch nearly every day with a boom box turned to nearly full volume in his lap, tuning the dial to a different rap/rock station mid-song every thirty seconds.

The garden saves me. It roots me in such an obvious way that it's funny. I dig my hands into that cucumberless soil, and my brain agrees that we'll give it another go. My brain agrees that I'm a writer, not an academic, although it will take me years to not consider myself a failure and then a few more before I circle back and teach in academia again anyway. I garden as obsessively as another person might seek talk therapy. Tomatoes, peppers, lettuce, looping scrolling squash vines, corn, columbine, daffodils, daisies. I garden the shit out of that little backyard.

After righthand side John dies, his daughter rents the house to a family friend, whose job as far as we can tell is to find all the money that suspicious-of-banks, Depression-era John has stashed in the walls and floors, which apparently is not a small sum. The family friend calls this money finding "renovating the house." We're also pretty sure this family friend is having an affair with a woman he insists on calling his "cleaning lady." The family friend is dead set on reclaiming the swath of improperly fenced yard. After I plant corn there he shoves a ladder in the middle and smashes the seedlings to bits.

The home we move to is close enough to our first one that we can walk some of our stuff up the hill and through our new front door. Before we buy the house, which isn't the first one we look at this time, we walk door-to-door introducing ourselves to potential neighbors. This is how we meet Roberta (Bert) and Mike, our soon-to-be excellent next-door neighbors, who porch sit like pros from the house Bert grew up in.

We lug along the potted plum tree, but I leave all the perennials behind. I start over again, digging up lawn from the long sloping yard and turning it into more garden each summer for the next twenty years.

Today the leaves shift into yellows and reds across our hilly neighborhood, and I harvest perky, bright green brussels sprouts and fill a basket with end-of-season tomatoes, a couple of late pattypan squashes, an armload of poblano peppers, parsley, kale, swiss chard, heirloom carrots, and the last of the zinnias for the kitchen table. I drop off a bag of vegetables to Bert, walk some over to Margaret.

I've planted myself where the steelworkers once took root. Amazing views rise up beyond our little house. Our neighbors share stories over fences and argue about parking. Many still live in the homes they grew up in, taking over the place like a giant relay race until there's no one left to pass it to and new people like us move in.

I've learned to cultivate my yard, my life, my relationships in this city. I've learned to be part of the fabric of a place instead of moving through and out of it. I've learned how to be comfortable in the skin of a writer on my own terms, to listen to my intuition, to lean on my creativity, to continue to plant the vegetables too close together.

It's all so fragile, the history of the food we grow, of the people we supplant. It gets lost in the shuffle of daily life as we dig in, as we try to leave or stay.

JADE PLANT

Weird shadows at the edges. A single overhead light burns. It seems like deep night but it's probably 7:00 p.m. in my kitchen. An unfinished jigsaw puzzle spreads out on the center island table. The table, a great score—found in an old building, half restored—looks like an island but then folds out to a big square. Perfect in the Before Times for seating six friends for a dinner party. But instead it's the During Times, late March, early April 2020. The time of a global pandemic. A time when whole months are unpindownable. The time of jigsaw puzzles.

I stand in the middle of my kitchen staring down at the puzzle pieces but not yet touching them. My phone, propped against a stack of books across the room, live-streams my friend Guy Capecelatro. He's playing a virtual concert via Facebook from his own living room in Kittery, Maine, in the new house he bought after he sold the house he and his wife Pam Raiford lived in for twenty years across the bridge in Portsmouth, New Hampshire. Pam died three years ago in April 2017. April 13th. I know the date because it's a Before Times time I'll never forget.

Guy sings, forcing himself to start over in this nice new house that I video toured but did not get to see in person because the pandemic hit and I ran out of time that I didn't know was limited.

Guy plays his guitar as we try out this new way to communicate without touching or breathing on each other. He sings a song he wrote for Pam called "All This Everything." It's from Pam's point of view. *I stuck around as long as I could, but I was already gone. I knew it would be harder for you, love, but I know you're strong.*

And it's true, I realize. Pam left us long before she was actually gone. She turned inward to focus on . . . dying. With grace and in a way she felt sure of after she stopped the chemo. This deep introspection meant she could only be concerned about us in a day-to-day benevolent omniscient narrator kind of way. She looked out over our lives as she stepped away and deep into her own. Pam funneled her last vestiges of outward energy into Guy. They'd been together for twenty-seven years, married for part of that time, but marriage was never the point. It was all about love and happiness. In fact, I watched them fall into each other one summer in the early '90s. As we all pushed movie videos into our players, played frisbee on the beach, ate cookies from Ceres Bakery, and made breakfast together on the weekends, they slid from friendship to couple. From ungrounded to happiness. Click. I witnessed them carve out a relationship based on helping each other and others, on supporting and cultivating passions and goals. Pam's face lit up every time Guy walked into the room; Guy snuggled her close on the couch as I visited each year.

Pam knew Guy wouldn't be alright after she was gone. "Can you watch out for Guy?" she asked my husband Rick the last day we saw her alive. "Make sure he's okay."

"You are an amazing friend" is the last thing Pam says to me. The afternoon sun leaks into her small, colorful living room, the walls lined with CDs and books. Other people wait just beyond the doorframe to see her, and we need to hit the road. Pam and I hug and clutch hands before we let go that last time, which, part of my brain can't admit, is the last time. We hold steady eye contact as she heads into something I can't possibly give advice about, which has been the center of our friendship—advising each other, about everything, always. I work hard to hold it together for her. I live six hundred miles away, and time is running out.

You are an amazing friend. I hold that sentence like it's a three-dimensional thing I can carry and touch. Sometimes in my mind what she said was, *You were an amazing friend.* I imagine Pam talking in past tense about herself to get me ready. But she wasn't.

She's there in the puffy, borrowed old-man recliner that has become her sick bed. She's dying, her cat perched, purring by her shoulder, Guy beside her logging medications. She's still there, my amazing friend.

The fall before this we orchestrate getting some of us to Seapoint Beach to swim, because Pam says she wants to swim. Afterward Pam and I take what will be our last walk on the little beach that has been our touchpoint for decades, with its grassy dunes and rocky shore. It's a silent walk, and Pam is bald from the chemo that she'll stop in January. "I feel like the chemo disconnects me from myself," she'll write in an email, ". . . I just really want to be as present in my mind and body, and to feel as genuinely me, as possible."

This day we have the warm air with a crisp edge, the seagulls circling. Waves swish to shore with their hypnotic shushes. We take slow steps, deep breaths, looking to the horizon.

"I'm scared," Pam suddenly says, turning to face me. We hug for a long time as she cries, our favorite world spread out all around us, friends gathered on a blanket in the distance.

"We'll get through this together," I say. "We will." Neither of us knows this isn't true. Pam will get through this alone. There's no other way.

Guy plays his song, and he doesn't cry, but I think he will once he clicks off. I'm crying though. I stand in my kitchen, a bright light shining sickly, illuminating these ridiculous three thousand puzzle pieces, arms at my sides, sobbing like a wronged toddler. I cry and cry and cry.

A month before Pam dies she gives me a jade plant that had once been my own jade plant that I gave her when I left Portsmouth, back when we all once miraculously lived within a couple block radius of each other. 1991, and I was en route to San Francisco via a three-month cross-country trip with my boyfriend. I gave away all my plants because there wasn't room for them in my car or my new life.

Pam had a place for the jade in her sunny high school classroom. I had no idea it still lived twenty-six years later, a giant jade stretching up out of a big blue pot. I strap it into my car's backseat with a seat belt and drive home to Pittsburgh.

I take a photo of the plant all buckled up and a second shot of it on a little wooden stand in a corner near my kitchen window. I text these images to Pam, and she writes back how happy she is to see the plant settled in.

For a time the plant becomes Pam. I stick a little Sculpey clay dinosaur earring that she made for me more than twenty-six years ago into the soil, and Rick pokes in a pretty feather we find on one of our morning walks through South Side Park. Transplanted baby Pams soon grow in pots beside the big one. Pam everywhere. The way it should be.

March 17, 2020, I dive into quarantine for real right after being lured into a last freelance work meeting in a small, enclosed conference room where a man tells me there is no way we'll quarantine, that people have important things to do and can't just stay home. There is no way *he* will quarantine. I nod, tired already, knowing he's wrong, understanding the virus from a doctor friend and my already obsessive internet reading about the 1918 pandemic and how it played out, coming in fast and haphazardly spiking as government officials argued about quarantine, masking, and treatment.

Pittsburgh didn't fare well back then. "The city suffered the highest per capita death rate in the nation, a fact that many historians blame on local leaders' reluctance to shut down the economy and a longstanding apathy toward the health of the general population," Bill O'Toole writes in "When the Spanish Flu Swept In, Pittsburgh Failed the Test" for an April 2020 feature in *Pittsburgh Quarterly*. I know, to a very small degree, what's coming, and I have the shopping lists and the masks and the bleach, gloves, and Clorox wipes to prove it. I convince friends to cancel readings and house concerts and just generally try to educate the people I love really fast. All along, my pandemic experience is about two weeks ahead of everyone else's, which is like having very stressful clairvoyance.

A few weeks after Pam dies in the Before Times, I stand in this same kitchen, crying. Not sobbing like a toddler, but instead tears leak steadily from my eyes as if I'm a cracked egg. Hands in my pockets, I aimlessly look out the big picture window onto the street that runs in front of our home. I sigh and tell myself I need to pull it together and then I leak some more. I'm at a standoff with myself. I can't fathom getting over Pam's death, and I don't want to. I feel a dull, throbbing despair. Then the song "Sherry" by Frankie Vallie plays on my Pandora station.

I've never heard this song in rotation on any of my many stations, and I don't notice it at first this day, deep into my introspection, but soon it nudges me from my wallowing revelry. I wait a minute, letting it sink in. Frankie and his high-pitched warbling, asking me if I'll come out tonight. And I laugh because it's so Pam to make that song play right then, to cheer me up, to let me know that there's some Pam-ness left in me, in the world, somewhere.

"Sorry," I imagine her saying. "I couldn't figure out exactly how post-death song projection worked, and I could only find 'Sherry,' but it does have your name in it, even if it's spelled wrong." Pam would laugh and shrug her shoulders. Lean forward, touch my knee, and laugh some more. "I'll work on it," she'd say.

It doesn't end there. I hear "Sherry" in the most unlikely places over the next year: At the Black Trumpet upstairs bar in Portsmouth the day before Pam's memorial service. On the alternative college radio station playing in my car. In my local grocery store shopping aisle. And each time I think: *Pam*.

Is it Pam? Does it matter? It works. It's Pam manifesting to me, just like she did in a dream soon after she died. She entered my sleeping consciousness as a large Black man. I'm guessing in Pam's goofy way this was also the only avatar she could figure out, so she just went with it. She walked into my dream as a lovely, tall Black man instead of her white, petite self, to let me know she was okay. Totally at peace. Everything was fine.

Light hits my bathroom window a certain way to make it glow. That's Pam too. Her death makes me understand faith, how people believe in Jesus Christ. It makes me wish I had it. Instead I worship at the altar of Pam, who brings me joy but who is not the son of God, for sure.

Things work in inexplicable ways, and perhaps we can't fully understand the inexplicable until we mourn, until we feel an energy existing after it isn't around anymore. Perhaps it's this mourning made acute by a global pandemic that pulls me to practice qigong. Fate, magic, coincidence—none of these ideas are new, but I'm in them, working it out.

I scroll through my Facebook feed on March 17, 2020, my nerves set on high and my house smelling like bleach. I notice that Moshe Sherman has decided to offer free, virtual thirty-minute qigong classes. Moshe and his wife Kate run an energetic healing business together called Cloud Gate. I don't know what qigong is, but I've met Moshe at parties because it's Pittsburgh, a big town small city, and everyone of a certain cultural and artistic ilk ends up meeting everyone eventually. That day, I'm as ungrounded as everyone else, so it appeals to me: doing some kind of stretching, not leaving my house, practicing this thing I don't understand every Wednesday, Thursday, and Friday.

I assume I'll be my typical self and do qigong a few times and then I'll move on. But something happens as the construct of time breaks down and the world becomes more day-less each day. I need activities to put a backbone in my week. Wednesday, Thursday, Friday is qigong from 8:30–9:00 a.m. Tuesday and Thursday evenings become tai chi, led by my friend James Simon. On Thursdays after tai chi, I tune into Guy, who plays a virtual concert for an hour, writing new songs every week and taking requests. These things—these events playing from my phone—become my gravity. They're the reason I need to know the day of the week. And when Moshe tells me to take a breath in four parts: the inhale, hold the full breath, and the exhale, hold the empty breath. I do. And that breathing tethers me to the ground of my kitchen, keeping me upright.

I soon find out that qigong is a series of breathing and stretching exercises. A qigong practitioner guides the qi, or spirit/wind/energy through their body, getting their spirit/wind/energy aligned. It's an ancient traditional Chinese medicine (TCM) rooted in Taoist thinking, but it's also sort of nothing. Qi itself can't be measured or easily defined, although scientists have tried. It's a physical and spiritual practice where action and belief merge to make a person feel better. Qigong is the only self-healing pillar of TCM, so it's perfect for quarantine. I become my own guide and healer, with Moshe as my super grounded and enthusiastic virtual cheerleader.

Qigong. I talk about it too much at first. So much that I give people fair warning: I'm going to bring it up again, I say. Not that it's the answer to everything, but it has been the answer to many things, for me, during this Time of During. One minute I stand in my kitchen sobbing while a jigsaw puzzle lays unmade before me and the next I stand in my kitchen with my phone propped on a shelf with Moshe telling me to spread my arms wide, to give myself a big hug. He tells me to say out loud, *I love myself completely*. He tells me to stretch my arms wide and then do it again. We raise our arms to the heavens as we inhale; we wiggle our fingers toward the sky as we hold the breath; we lower our arms exhaling; we wiggle our toes as we hold the breath. It's hard to explain how helpful this is. The centering that qigong does is nearly immediate. I'm breathing; I'm loving myself; I'm startling my lymph nodes into action with some tapping up and down my arms, in my armpits, up and down my legs, tapping across my chest. This tapping tells our bodies to get going, it guides our energy so that it circulates, whether we are personally circulating or not.

I feel alive.

I can only practice qigong when it's live with Moshe. This only becomes a problem from Saturday to Tuesday when he doesn't offer a live virtual class. I could watch old classes. They're available on Cloud Gate's Facebook page. But I don't because I need human contact even if it's virtual. And I suffer for it. I lose it from Saturday through Tuesday and then it's Wednesday morning and I'm reborn again.

Moshe wears glasses that turn automatically to sunglasses in an aviator style that was popular in the late '70s. He has puffy hair, wears tie-dye T-shirts, and does goofy things like saying hi to his toes when he wiggles them. He says, "Hi toes!" and then he has his toes say, "Hi Moshe!" He makes qigong unserious. I click a couple of heart icons as we end for the day.

After Pam dies I look for some of the hundreds of letters and postcards we wrote to each other over the years, seeing as how our day-to-day friendship ended in 1991 when I moved away. I find a postcard that must have been tucked in with a present. She says it's a cold winter dusk and that she's rushing to get it to the post office. "I wish you were here with me," she writes, "and we were going to sit by a warm N.H. fire and drink wine and talk for hours. I love you, Sherrie." She signs it Pam with a big looping *P*. Always she tells me she loves me. Always. It's just a short note, but it takes me back to that small New England town, how beautiful the light can be at dusk, the sound of tugboats and buoys clanging in the harbor, crisp crunchy snow all around, Pam rushing with her purposeful stride, all skirt, scarf, tights, boots, long hair, stocking cap bobbing and moving with her messenger bag slung crosswise, my present addressed and tucked inside. Waving to friends she passes, saying, "I gotta go! See you soon! Love you!"

Pam writes in another card with a big field of sunflowers on the front: "I feel at peace in the world with you by my side, so well understood. I feel very lucky to have you in my life, to feel close and connected to you no matter how much time or distance separates us."

We were amazing friends. And because of that, when Pam dies part of me goes with her. Our history, all the ongoing subjects we examined on our beach walks. All the confessions we made to each other. Those things are with her, and gone. There are times now when I have a realization about something—just recently about an old boyfriend, for instance. I had a huge realization about him and the way he treated me one night years ago that probably led to a lot of problems for me, but I hadn't realized it until that very moment. My brain immediately puts it onto a list of things to tell Pam the next time I see her. We'll work it through from every angle. She'll process it and then tell me something that will be incredibly helpful to me understanding it in the bigger context of my life.

A second later I understand I have no one to tell it to. I mean, of course I have friends, but I would have to give backstory and set it up and explain the ex-boyfriend from decades ago, and it would be exhausting for me and maybe exhausting for them, and I just don't really *want* to do that. The chapter of our ongoing shared analysis of what it meant to live in this world is over. It's gathered up and stored in me, sealed shut, like a time capsule.

There are days I look at Pam the Jade Plant in the corner and I'm just so weirdly sad that the real Pam isn't living through this historic pandemic and coming up with amazing, relevant, online teaching solutions for her high school history classroom. She would have absolutely been all over it. Reading up on the 1918 pandemic and making connections. She would have been a solid grounding force for everyone through it all.

There's Guy, still here in this world, alone in his new house, playing a concert for me on a Thursday night. "Hi Sherrie. Great to see you here," he says after I click a little heart and type, "Hi Guy!" in the comments.

I work as a copy editor for a woman who believes Andy Warhol communicates with her from the afterworld. Artist Madelyn Roehrig spent eight years filming Warhol's grave, collecting and photographing notes and objects people left for him for the project *Figments: Conversations with Andy*. I helped with the final edits of the first of four catalogs representing each season, this one for winter, *Andy, Can You Hear Us?* Madelyn tells me that she thinks Andy heard her when she needed late-stage editing help, and my name came to mind, so she sent me a note on Facebook.

Madelyn first understood the possibility of communicating with the dead after the death of her own son Jon. When *Figments* began she lived near Warhol's gravesite just outside of Pittsburgh in Bethel Park, Pennsylvania. She regularly visited and photographed the headstone and the people who came to see Andy (as she calls him, never

Warhol). Her visits and early videos and photography work led to Madelyn asking Andy for advice on her visits, and soon he helped her make decisions about her creative projects and MFA thesis. Throughout the catalog there are reproduced notes written by visitors to Andy thanking him, asking him questions, wondering about him, and wanting to be his friend. There are photographs of decorated soup cans, wigs, candles, dolls, bananas, and drawings that people have left behind as offerings.

The catalog comes out in August 2020, and I mask up and head to the St. John the Baptist Byzantine Catholic Cemetery where Warhol is buried. I've lived in Pittsburgh for over twenty years and have worked on many writing and editing projects with The Andy Warhol Museum on Pittsburgh's North Side, yet I've never been to Warhol's gravesite. It's in the suburbs of all places, a completely unlikely place for an eccentric, blue-movie-producing pop artist to rest eternally. There's a smooth green slope of lawn and, up a hill, some understated headstones. He's there, resting with his mom, dad, and brother. This day, there are Campbell's Soup Cans scattered about and both an Elvis impersonator and a man dressed as Warhol himself with a black pandemic bandana mask. I get a couple of catalogs from Madelyn and mask-chat with some women involved with the project, take some pictures, and then I walk away.

This idea of communicating with the dead is nothing new. The Victorians were very into it, of course. Spiritualism took the dead by storm. Séances, Ouija boards, visits with mediums, and images from spirit photographers took center stage in living rooms and at lecterns across the country in the nineteenth century. Marie Curie, William James, Mae West, Thomas Edison, and Mary Todd Lincoln all believed. My mother and her sisters had a Ouija board in the 1940s. A fellow baker, Christopher Fortier once used a Ouija board in the early '90s to have a chat with a ghost at Ceres Bakery, a sailor who

Chris says followed him home and yanked on his ankles when it was time for him to get up for his baking shift. The Ouija communication was to tell him to stop it, that Chris could wake up on his own just fine, thanks. And it worked.

We experienced many ghostly machinations at Ceres Bakery in the years I worked there. In fact, the bakery and the building next door, the Sheafe Street Inn, show up on hauntedhouses.com and other Portsmouth ghost walk tours. I personally yelled for the ghost—whose dim shadow I thought I could sometimes see in my peripheral vision—to cut it out more than once during my late-night bread shifts as the egg wash bowl zipped across the baking table or the coffeemaker turned off then on then off again.

In the late nineteenth century "somewhere between four million and eleven million people identified as Spiritualists in the United States alone," writes Casey Cep in her 2021 *New Yorker* article, "Why Did So Many Victorians Try to Speak with the Dead?" "Some of the leaders back then were hucksters, and some of the believers were easy marks, but the movement cannot be dismissed merely as a collision of the cunning and the credulous," she asserts. The rise of Spiritualism for Victorians followed the rise of industrialization. The ready availability of cheap, printed information, the rise in population as industrial cities established themselves, and a high infant mortality rate created the perfect ghost storm. "It's counter-intuitive really, because Spiritualism is typically thought of as other-worldly and magical, but I think it actually makes us more aware of where objects come from—how they don't, in fact, materialize out of thin air, but there's a story behind them. There's a rich symbolism there," notes Professor Aviva Briefel, who argues that industrialization led to the rise of manufactured objects and the scrutinizing of those objects, some of which made it possible to try and capture otherworldliness—cameras, for example. In Victorian séances, manufactured chairs, tables, musical instruments, and lamps knocked on the floor, rattled, tapped, and flew around the room, *becoming* the dead, stretching their everyday purpose into the world of the unknown.

Today in the midst of a technology boom, as Facebook, Zoom, FaceTime, TikTok, and other social media platforms make the impossible possible, there's a resurgence in beyond-death communication. "Almost a third of Americans say they have communicated with someone who has died, and they collectively spend more than two billion dollars a year for psychic services on platforms old and new," Cep writes. Spiritualists, like the concept of qi, have never had a quick and easy definition for themselves. The movement has always embraced just about anyone who wants to connect with someone beyond the grave, however they want to do it. These days Facebook memorials pop up on pages, and the social media site sometimes becomes a medium for communicating with the deceased, the person's social media presence existing as an entity beyond the self. "Many people have a strong social presence that lingers after their biological death in the same way that people who are physically alive have experienced a 'social death' and no longer have an embodied corporeal [online] presence, due to an illness," writes Jocelyn M. DeGroot in her dissertation "Reconnecting with the Dead via Facebook: Examining Transcorporeal Communication as a Way to Maintain Relationships."

Some people believe messages posted to Facebook memorials are received even if there isn't a response from the deceased person, and who am I to argue against this? What is a self anyway? Is my avatar me? Who do we think we are? The connection between the body and the mind—not a new problem to work out. All of this is just a new way to think about communication and existence.

Pam's ashes are let loose by Guy at Seapoint Beach in Kittery, Maine. Pam is in a Tupperware container—which she would have hated—and then she's floating free in the Atlantic along with some pretty flowers, and we all hold hands with our feet on the hard sand, without her. Pam, Pam, Pam everywhere as we walk down to the rocky point and back.

Life feels good that day. I feel a catharsis wash over us. "Okay," I think. "Okay. Thank you, Pam." We're all thinking this. We aren't thinking, fuck ovarian cancer. We aren't angry. We're trying to find ways to be kinder, because that's what Pam wants from us, and it's the least we can do as she floats away into forever.

I wake up from a colossal nap because I hear Moshe talking in my dream. In reality it's Moshe on a local NPR radio program playing on my phone. He says he's grateful. In keeping with the confusion of the During Times, my dreams have incorporated qigong as the radio journalist interviews Moshe about qigong, and I realize that *qi*—a word I've been using in Scrabble for decades—is the first part of qigong. I knew it meant some kind of wind, but I didn't understand its essential importance to energy work and this practice I've started, didn't for a second make the connection to the indispensable, killer Scrabble word until Moshe takes the time to define it. Life force. We're transforming life force energy, shifting it from here to there, the *there* being someplace better. A better way of feeling and living.

Before pandemic times I meet up with my friend Brittany Hailer—Brit—for a tarot card reading. It's a few months after Pam dies. We decide to get together at Kelly's Bar. We drink and do tarot and catch up. Brit, a writer, editor, and young old soul who sets out jars of water to charge during full moons has loads of dark brown hair piled on top of her head and a mischievous lip-sticked smile as she lays out the cards on the Formica tabletop in the dim light of the bar, a beer at her elbow, a candle flickering in its tall glass container.

She takes a moment to look them over, and the color drains from her face. She hems and haws and says she sees some weird stuff—maybe it has to do with death? I tell her about Pam. I talk about

"Sherry" and describe carting the jade plant home. I mention the sparkling light that seems to follow me around these days and how Pam decided to make decisions about her death instead of following medical protocol. How it seems her strength in life has transferred to a strength in death too.

The cards continue to freak Brit out, and later—much later—she tells me that she thinks Pam followed her that night. That she could feel Pam there before she started her car. I imagine Pam curiously following Brit, wondering if maybe Brit could manifest her, for just a second, to say, "I'm gone but still here. I love you!" I imagine Pam trying to tell Brit something to tell me before she fades back into the ether, but she can't figure out how to do it. And Brit just sits there, channeling Pam-ness, breathing in and out her soft but fierce energy.

Later still I give a baby Pam jade plant to Brit as a housewarming present. She keeps the plant right by her computer as she works. Within a year it doubles in size.

Qigong isn't something that I would have been interested in during other, more cynical stages of my Gen-X life. I think it's a post-Pam receptivity to the energies of the world that opens me up to this practice, and in doing so lets me vibrate a little better as Sherrie. When I start to think it through, just about everything is amazing and impossible. Sight. Hearing. Taste. A friend playing a house concert inside a phone. Warhol's gravesite covered in soup cans. Ouija boards. Houseplants. Why not be amazed at the negative space a person leaves behind when she dies? Why not believe in the energy we can't see but can maybe move through our bodies? What's gained by not believing this?

Qi "is neither created nor is it ever destroyed; it simply changes in its manifestation," states the Earl E. Bakken Center for Spirituality and Healing at the University of Minnesota. It's this idea of the eternal that also straddles all religions, the elusive that drives us nuts as humans trying to overthink it all. The Taoist basis of qigong doesn't distinguish between the physical and spiritual world. Qi joins the mind and body. One can't exist without the other, yin and yang, positive and negative. It's foundational, these opposites. Qi isn't something that's prescribed or even grounded in reality, which tends to be not cool in the Western world where we want answers, prescriptions in milligrams, and at minimum a double-blind clinical trial.

But what if there aren't answers? What if that's the whole point? What if we can communicate with the dead? What if they can communicate with us? It isn't even that weird. Sometimes I talk to my houseplants, just rest in the beauty of all the living things I've acquired since the pandemic. They line the front windows of my kitchen, hang from my ceiling, rest shoulder to shoulder along my window sills. We all just sit around waiting for the next thing to happen, humming into our lives, our clocks on different timetables.

I drive toward Edgewood, a borough right outside Pittsburgh's Squirrel Hill Tunnel, take an exit, round a curve, and then journey up a narrow slope to get to Kate Sherman's Cloud Gate office for a shiatsu massage. Kate, small and elf-like, is fair-skinned with straight, limp hair and a sweet smile. She's in touch with a lot of things most of us can't see. That's clear to me right away. She strikes me as a tiny person who could lift a car. I lie down on the thin mat spread out on her floor, and she covers me with a sheet. The sun shines outside, and I can dimly hear the sounds of the neighborhood through the windows. Kate works her way around my body using her hands on my pressure points. There's a moment when I distinctly feel the energy humming around my body. Zap. The qi, although I can't yet name it. She kneels at my head with her hands on my lower neck, and a big bright ball appears in what I guess is my third eye because my real eyes are closed. We just sit there for a little while. And then she stands up and hits a gong at the other end of the room. The second the mallet hits the metal, a big white ball of light turns into a big red heart. A big red heart. In my head. But I can see it. With my eyes closed.

I'm just telling you what happened.

"Wow. I was seeing rainbows and unicorns and puppies," Kate says once I open my eyes and get myself together. She echoes what others have told me over the years—that my energy is intense and strong, and my aura is huge. It's a powerful thing to be told this after having just manifested a heart in my brain.

The first time I meet Kate she snakes her way through a crowded party at my friend James Simon's sculpture studio loft. It's packed—a true Before Times event. A band plays, and heaps of food and empty wine bottles line the counters. People dance near the front of the room in the dim light. Through James's third-floor windows, Downtown Pittsburgh twinkles in the distance. I sit on a stool in the kitchen area, and Kate walks up holding a small plastic container of blueberries. She cups them like an offering.

Connections we can see and not see are out there all over the place in the present, past, and future. We pull the meaning together. Sometimes it takes years. Sometimes it speaks to us, and sometimes we miss it altogether.

Pam the person and the plant are dead by March 21, 2023. Almost six years since Pam my friend died, her plant namesake takes its last gasp. It isn't sudden. Pam the Jade Plant fades away and never revives, although I try everything. She bore so much plant responsibility these past years. The plant's time had come. Pam was done, tired, and drooping.

She leaves behind four healthy little jades in my kitchen to start a new legacy. Guy also has a Pam, as does my friend Nancy, and

Brittany's Pam needs repotting again. It's the second much lesser death of Pam. One I'm ready for. I move her dinosaur earring to another smaller pot. I make a space for time to move us on. I don't feel Pam right near me anymore. I like to think she thinks I'm nearly ready to go it alone. I'm ready to shift my energy, to enter a new stage.

I look out the big picture window into the morning light. One car and then another blips by on our narrow street, each making their way to work out in an opened-up world. The pigeons peck at the birdseed in the driveway. A grasshopper in my little front yard, a big one, awkwardly makes a long arc across the window, hopping one way and then back the other. Then it hops right onto the glass, looking at me for just a second, and clumsily falls back to the grass. I think, *Pam*.

CARETAKER, MURDERER, UNDERTAKER

Dirt rounds the ridges under my fingernails, making crusty silver moons. I try to clean up before going out, but once I'm settled at the restaurant I look at my hands and start picking at the crud. There's a smear of green on my calf, a smudge of yellow on my skirt. I tuck the hem under my thigh. What is that? I don't know, but I know where it came from.

When people who don't garden think of gardens, I imagine they imagine straight lines, tidy vegetables, and reasonable, reliable, hoed dirt. I see them seeing a steady, predictable rate of cultivation that leads to their lunch, dinner, and future snacks.

But that isn't how gardeners garden. When I close my eyes and think about my garden, I inhale a glorious jumble of earth and rot and chaos. I see baskets of tomatoes, bushels of green beans. I exhale.

In my garden, things reseed—borage, cilantro, dill. They do this here and there in convenient and inconvenient places. They also do it unpredictably from year to year. There are multiple planted patches of carrots, broccoli, kale, and swiss chard. Too many tomato plants are staked and strapped to the fence. Volunteer butternut squash vines creep through the arugula. Perennial flowers—lilies and irises, echinacea and black-eyed Susans—pop up each season in the middle of the vegetables and herbs. Blackberries loop and cane themselves into the tiger lilies, into the potato bin. There are some straight rows, yes. But that isn't the point.

What is the point? I'm not sure, but it's something instinctual. Some kind of primal drive to fill and create and make flourish and then—well—kill and eat all that stuff that comes from the ground.

A gardener is a caretaker, murderer, and undertaker. We work toward death. On the way to harvest we drown bugs and chase groundhogs. We throw rocks. We actually throw rocks. We make elaborate deer deflectors with Irish Spring soap and tin pie pans and human hair. And then we put everything to rest and begin again.

Hearing my neighbor shoot the bunny with a BB gun? Honestly? I'm relieved. The bunnies are too cute for me. The bunnies win every time in my garden, but not in my neighbor's, and for that I am thankful.

I remember the first time I actually wanted to strangle a deer with my bare hands. It had daintily consumed all of my hard-to-grow, heartbreakingly beautiful, light yellow, heart-shaped heirloom tomatoes right off the vine, leaving just the vine—vibrant green and inedible. No tomatoes.

Even a baby deer. I would have strangled it.

I'm a vegetarian. You need to understand that these garden impulses are impulses that pulse outside of my ethics. In my real life I type on a computer. I listen to NPR. I cook a lot and can set up a mean *mise en place* on my cutting board. I play ukulele and drink red wine and Manhattans. I read books, play Scrabble. I stay pretty clean. Wear lipstick when I get dressed up. I don't touch spiders. I squeal when I see a snake or a mouse. I don't believe in the death penalty or animal cruelty or guns.

But still. I want to destroy that which destroys my kingdom.

This past year, I let a carrot go to seed in giant, flowering, amoeba-like blooms. These tendrils looked aquatic out there as they bobbed and ducked at the chicken wire fence so uncarrot-like. I couldn't bear to pull it up. It grew and grew, and now it will become next year's carrots—reincarnation. I am god here. But I'm not religious either.

Gardening has created in me a kind of fevered unleashing, an opening up. I kill the bugs that try to kill my vegetables and then I kill the vegetables, too, and eat them.

If I had a redo, if I had one of those chances to change that you sometimes read about—*A lawyer becomes a baker! An accountant becomes a rock star!*—I would become a farmer. It would change me totally. I understand this.

In the garden, as I work, big bumblebees and skinny honeybees hum beside me. In a frenzy they poke every single bloom in sight. They are ecstatic over the sunflowers this year. They are, I am certain, orgasming on the sunflowers. I've never seen anything like it, except maybe at that one party in New Hampshire in 1989.

And then it's a gloriously sunny midsummer day—spears of sunlight sneak down through the sorghum leaves as I thin the beets. That's when I see the spider—I mean, this is a giant arachnid. She has housed herself in the brussels sprouts plant with an elaborate, cone-like web. I learn later that she's an orb weaver. Right now she is furry and mighty and waving her many arms at me as if to say: GET OUT. With only an ounce of a shudder, with zero squeal, I say to myself, "Good. That's good. She's *good*. A good guy. Mean, but good." And I keep working. Same with the giant, robotic-faced praying mantis. Same with the thin black snake I see slithering down under the raspberry bushes. *Good guys*. Good.

I reach for a tomato, and my thumb plunges into the splotchy moldy goo that covers its underside. I wipe my hand on my shorts. Later, when I'm inside, my hands will be coated in yellow pollen as if the garden has gilded me, changed my skin into pollen-dusted sandpaper.

Tiny, bulleted gold eggs make a tidy triangle on the back of my zucchini leaves. I rip the leaf and drown the eggs. I smoosh and smear until I feel feral. Bowls of beer drown the slugs. We call the bowls slug parties. We do.

Sometimes when I come inside sweaty and dazed, I look at myself in the mirror and, for a moment, I don't know who I am. My eyes have become electric blue, and I am so alive with dirt and life that I glow.

I know if I were a farmer and not just this urban-gardener-on-a-slightly-larger-scale, I would eat meat. I would have to. I would grow cows and chickens, and how would they eventually be so different from the vegetables I kill on a daily basis? How would wringing one of their necks be different from twisting an ear of corn from its stalk? Some days my hands tingle with this knowledge. The power of cultivation. The power of knowing life and death. BAM—I smash the cucumber beetle against the wooden post. SNIP—I get that cabbage moth before it flits away.

I transport a ladybug gently, carefully, over to the green beans, and I drown hundreds of stink bugs in soapy water each early morning. The dew glistens on the grass, and my little Yorkie runs to bark at our next-door neighbor, again. The bee balm and chamomile sway in the breeze. A neurotic hummingbird takes a big interest in the balm's bright red petals. Darting, darting. Traffic from Downtown Pittsburgh's commuters zips and unzips on the parkways down the hill. They inch along like the ants on my peony buds. The crickets kick in, sounding like tiny car alarms.

I do feel bad some days for all of those stink bugs. I do. In general I am a kind and generous person. But just today I saw a troop of tiny stink bugs on my scarlet runner beans and I said out loud: "Get the fuck away from my beans."

I harvest the vegetables, and I make delicious, fresh meals and canned goods for my husband and friends. I compost what is left over after the prep. Those leftovers break down and rot in the big black container in my yard until they aren't recognizable. Until they pass over to become nutritious dirt. Healthy, beautiful compost that I spread across the beds as I get ready for the next growing season. Always cycling everything around in a big, heaving, wriggling worm-filled circle that brings me back to life.

INSTINCTS

It's 1980, and I tie my sneakers and tighten the drawstring on my baggy sweatpants that cinch with elastic at the ankles. I zip up one of my brother's hooded sweatshirts over my long underwear top, wrap a scarf around my neck, and pull on a stocking cap. I can see my breath as I jog down the gravel driveway and turn right onto the sidewalk that traces Darlington Road, the main thoroughfare through Patterson Township. I swing my arms and dodge bumps and cracks in the uneven terrain where I once rode my red tricycle and then my red, white, and blue banana seat bicycle. My best friend Jill Smith and I have started jogging. She begins at her house. We meet in the middle and then jog back to one or the other's to eat snacks and watch TV.

This jogging craze is new for us, fairly new to the United States, and I'm unsure why we've jumped on this bandwagon, but in two years, instead of this I'll pop a Jane Fonda aerobic workout cassette into my boombox and bounce around in my bedroom while wearing legwarmers. I try to follow Fonda's perky voice and the accompanying booklet directions that have me reaching, kicking, and lifting.

My heart rate increases. I look for Jill's outline jogging toward me, dressed in a nearly identical getup. Along the route I'll hear a truck or car honk. *Honk-honk* or just one quick tap. These honks come from men. I know this. I come to expect three to four honks in the span of my jogging route. At the time I think the honks are a yes vote. I want honks because that's how it works. Women exist, and men honk at them if they're pretty. These honks and catcalls become a background to my new teen life. I'm thirteen years old.

Mill towns focus on the strong body—the figuring-out of the world with one's hands. The grunt, the pull. It's no wonder that the region where I was born gave forth so many football stars.

Growing up in Beaver Falls, I sometimes felt like a movie extra in real time. In fact, the fictitious town Ampipe in 1983's *All the Right Moves*, which starred Tom Cruise, was based on a mix of dying Western Pennsylvania mill towns like mine, and this kind of movie has come to reflexively define the place, as pop culture is wont to do. It's a white-male, jock-centered world.

Yet Western Pennsylvania is where my own particular feminism took root, a philosophy not based in academic theory or intellectualism. My autonomy arose from toughness of place. Outside of my quiet family home boomed a loud-talking world where people yelled good-natured banter across a room, where the lived experience was external and in my face. My ideas, formed by the aggressive nature of the communication around me, turned into a kind of everyday, homemade feminism that assumed women were strong and didn't take any shit.

The jogging mania Jill and I are a part of sprang out of the landmark 1972 Title IX decision, which among many other things gave women access to participation in high school and college sports. By 1975 women were still only permitted to run a maximum of one mile in competition. But by 1982 my high school has girls participating in cross country, and I'm running the 400 and 1600 relays, long jumping, high jumping, and lettering on the Blackhawk High School track and field team.

Born in 1967, I was an infant in the beginning decade of second-wave feminism, America's sexual revolution. As I came into teenhood, sexuality dripped from the subtextual pores of the TV I consumed, the magazines I read, and the billboards I watched zip by as I sat unseat-belted in the passenger seat of my mom's brand-new Cutlass Ciera.

Second-wave feminism demanded autonomy for (white) (middle-class) adult women, and soon, probably not coincidentally, the movie and advertising industry shifted away from the getting-more-difficult-to-handle, of-age curvy bombshell to nearly-flat-chested little girls whose sexual identity was up for grabs. Exit: Jayne Mansfield. Enter: Brooke Shields, older than me by two years.

Shields was fifteen when her Calvin Klein TV ads and billboards slammed into popular culture like a sex-filled, tight-denimed tsunami. In the commercials, soon banned by several networks but aired enough to become instantly iconic, Richard Avedon's camera lingers, slowly revealing Shields's body.

Here she poses in a stark, empty room. The camera notes her leather boots, traces the leg of her jeans, then angles toward Shields's open crotch and western belt buckle. She softly whistles "Oh, My Darling Clementine" as the camera continues to her cuffed, loose, tucked-in dress shirt. Her long hair hangs to the side as she props a hand on her forehead, gazing at the floor, alone, autonomous, then a quick shift of the eyes to meet the camera and Shields asks, "You wanna know what comes between me and my Calvins?" Pause a beat. "Nothing."

"It was fun, innocent and yes, sexy as hell," Calvin Klein told *People* magazine in March 2023. Cool and smart, the ads whipped American consumers into a frenzy. I also wanted nothing between me and my Calvin Klein jeans.

It wasn't just Shields, who was also cast as a child prostitute in *Pretty Baby* at age eleven and a nearly-always-naked teen in *Blue Lagoon* at age fifteen. Jodie Foster's girl prostitute in *Taxi Driver* and Drew Barrymore's notorious real life gave the impression that young girls wanted it, that we were dangerous white-girl sirens calling young and old white guys to bed. My friends and I weren't even legally permitted to watch these movies. We were just the fallout. My desirability—my young Lolitaesque vixenness—was my fault. But I also couldn't help it. Somehow. Feminist autonomy led to my right to be obliviously irresistible, possibly naked on screen, not prudish. It was time to loosen up. Everything goes. Everything went. Studio 54 called, along with all the other discos spinning mirrored balls across the country, stealing gay and Black cultural tropes, making everything seem like good, clean, sexy fun.

Women weren't allowed to run over a mile in competition because our internal organs were too delicate or we were too delicate or we just couldn't handle it, depending on what you read, never mind that women had been birthing babies on the open plains and then carrying said babies on their backs for the rest of the trip for forever.

Second-wave feminists wanted sexual equality, not honks, or at least sexual equality and honks on their own terms. The Pill liberated us, sure. But maybe the idea of sexual freedom accommodated the patriarchy a little too much . . . ?

Feminism is really all about power. Equity. Sex can get a person sidetracked. What I want is to be able to talk without being interrupted. I want equal pay. I want men to stop stealing my ideas and taking credit for them. I want to be actually equal to men via the legislative and cultural eyes of my country, which seems like a ridiculously low bar. But incredibly we're still fighting this battle. The Equal Rights Amendment, which would have provided legal equity of the sexes and prohibited discrimination for all things, not just sex-sex, conceived of in 1923 and passed by Congress in 1972, has not been ratified as of May 2023.

Although I had read the entire *Little House on the Prairie* series, *Little Women*, all of Judy Blume's books, and, weirdly, Erma Bombeck, I remember sitting in my sophomore year high school creative writing class thinking, with some trepidation, that only white men could be real creative writers. Dead white men, which was, of course, confusing. And not true. But I hadn't met a writer or attended a reading, nor did I have an example of a day-to-day creative life to work from, and yet: I wanted it. And for some reason, probably having to do with Robert Frost, I thought I had to go to New England to get it.

My high school English teacher, Mr. Moore, recommended the University of New Hampshire because Charles Simic taught there, and Moore had surreptitiously given me *The Young American Poets*, the 1968 anthology edited by Paul Carroll, which includes Simic and a bunch of other radical contemporary poets of the time. Mr. Moore also introduced me to the poetry of Lawrence Ferlinghetti and Allen Ginsberg. I was probably the only tenth grader in all of Beaver County reading and writing papers on beat poetry.

Mr. Moore, Mr. Dattilo, Mr. Stevenson, and Mr. Cole taught a mix of English literature and history classes at Blackhawk High School. They all looked like they would have been more comfortable not wearing ties and poly-blend slacks, like they might have liked to put on some jeans and sit in a field, listening to Crosby, Stills, Nash, and Young or Joan Baez, but they stood in the hallways each day, dedicated to and bemused by the students swarming around them. Each encouraged me to be whomever I wanted to be. They didn't think it was outlandish for me to want to be a creative writer.

It was a happy accident that the school itself opened in 1973 and that these new hires attended college in the '60s, a time when education theory encouraged teachers to beef up intellectual curiosity and hone critical thinking skills using primary sources. Their experiences—traveling internationally, hopping trains over summer break—and their pedagogy—playing traditional Peruvian music on a cassette player before World Cultures class started, showing Monty Python films to help explain medieval times, and field-tripping students to see *Death of a Salesman* in Pittsburgh—became creative examples to me of what life could be like beyond high school.

By the mid-1980s the bottom had fallen out of the steel industry in my region, and the women workers were some of the first to be let go, along with many of the strides they had made in workplace equity. In a scene from the 1985 documentary *Women of Steel*, co-produced by Steffi Domike, Beth Destler, Linny Stovall, and Allyn Stewart, a group of Black and white unemployed women workers meet for beers at Chiodo's Tavern near Homestead Works, about five miles southeast of Pittsburgh. The camera pans from a billboard that reads "Feel the Velvet Canadian," where a wispy blond-haired white woman in a strapless black velvet dress lies across the span of the scaffolding, her arm draped over a bottle of whiskey, chin on her hand, staring seductively out into Homestead's gray skies. The camera continues down to starkly contrast Chiodo's, a worker's bar, and its simple brick exterior. It moves into the interior where the women, wearing T-shirts and jeans, smoke and chat. An open bag of Snyder's potato chips and pitchers of beer line the table. "A girl is raised to be nice, be a nice little girl, you know, and smile," says one woman, "and I found out the more I fought back with them, the more they respected me."

". . . All of a sudden she finds herself in a situation where she's the mother, the father, the breadwinner and everything else," another worker responds. "And that's when she's got to start becoming a fighter. The smile doesn't get it."

Later in the film a former steelworker gets ready for her shift at Pizza Hut. Working for lower wages with fewer protections and longer hours, she's relieved to have found any job in the flood of regional unemployment. She curls her hair with a curling iron, checks it in the bathroom mirror, and slides on her uniform visor.

That same year, 1985, I wear my cheerleading sweater and skimpy skirt and green and white saddle shoes to school on game days. I make good luck letters for the football and basketball players, give them a snack, and decorate their lockers each week. The cheerleaders paint signs to inspire the guys to WIN, and then the guys smash through them on their way onto the football field, onto the basketball court. We cheer and clap and jump and flip on the sidelines. *Shoot two.* Clap. Clap. Clap. *Shoot two.*

Blackhawk home football games, played on a field in rural Darlington, Pennsylvania, five miles north of the school, are a community event. Cars and pickup trucks snake along the winding roads from every borough and township in the area. Fellow students hawk programs on the lane into the stadium. Cows stand nearby. Fall nights, the stadium lights beam down through the mist onto the field. The band plays fight songs, tight and fast, as the cheerleaders kick and chant. I love being part of this big functioning organism, the feeling of thriving inside it. *Down the field. Over the line. Make. That. Score.*

For four years I'm a cheerleader. I like it, and I'm good at it. We choreograph routines to David Bowie's "Let's Dance," "Crazy Train" by Ozzy Osbourne, and "Ease on Down the Road," from *The Wiz.* I diligently date the captain of the football team my freshman and sophomore years.

But the world is changing, locally and nationally. In *Working Class Without Work: High School Students in a De-industrializing Economy,* Lois Weis reports her experience of following a group of high school students living in a formerly mill-centered town. It's 1985, and the mill's closing means the white boys at Freeway High can't expect to easily get factory jobs to serve as sole providers for their future families. No matter; they double down into demanding a patriarchal role anyway. "Now that males cannot envision a future of well-paying wage labor infused with traditional working-class definitions of masculinity, what is it they do have?" asks Weis. "It is clear . . . that males are not contemplating new forms of gender identity but are rearticulating, in a highly virulent fashion, the old forms of female domination." Reading Weis's insights into the future of these Gen Xers abandoned by industry, today, feels eerily predictive: she suggests the white men's disillusion with the evaporated union culture will shift them to embrace the New Right.

The white girls see some cards on the table, though, and when they think about it they're open to the idea of becoming more than a subordinate wife and homemaker, but they can't quite articulate what that means. The boys dig deeper into their roles, their sexist and racist language and actions increase within the school's social tiers. "For the white males portrayed here, blacks are 'others.' African American young men are a threat," Michael W. Apple writes in the introduction for the book. "For these same white-male youth, young white women aren't 'other'; they are 'less than.' They are inferior and should be subjected to male control."

By my senior year in 1985, the social structure of Blackhawk High School—and my role within it—begins to fracture as the steel industry in the region comes to a stop. As my friends and I ask ourselves why men's football and basketball get all the attention, we also start to annoy and aggravate the jocks. Previously only those two sports teams garnered homemade signs, but fellow cheerleader and homecoming queen Kati Csoman remembers, "We were a big hit [with the other athletes] for making signs for all of the sports that we hung in the gym." We even made one for the girls' cross-country team she reminds me via text late one night. "We were definitely all greatly impacted by our friendship," she continues.

Kati became a dean of international studies and has traveled worldwide with her husband, Emil, and son, Otto. Back in high school, she lived on the other end of Darlington Road. The Csoman household was loud and chaotic and full of bowls of hot peppers that Endre, Kati's father, grew in his garden.

My father sold life insurance to Endre Csoman and many others in the tight-knit Hungarian immigrant community. Endre had fled Hungary when he was eighteen, part of a giant exodus as the Soviets invaded during the Cold War. Sponsored to the United States by the First Hungarian Reformed Church of Pittsburgh in Hazelwood, he worked at Mayer China in Beaver Falls for nearly a decade, then B&W, then Koppel Steel. He was laid off while we were in high school.

After the layoff, "he worked painting, mostly, or other jobs," Kati tells me. "I do remember that we had a car that was pretty old and big, and I probably found it a little embarrassing. My mom ran out of gas on the hill coming out of Darlington after a football game one time—pretty late, like 11:00 p.m. I was embarrassed and pissed. My mom probably didn't have enough money to get gas. I remember that a lot. Finite resources at certain times. No cushion, so to speak. I was acutely aware of a limited financial situation at home, but my parents were wonderful at not inhibiting our experiences in any way."

There were seven of us that hung out together. The group included cheerleaders, football players, a wrestler, and some non-jocks. This co-ed jumble of friends annoyed the dominant clique of jocks. We messed with protocol, able to do so because many of us were technically members of the jock social group in the rigid school hierarchy. We were supposed to go to their keg parties, inhabit their values and priorities; we were supposed to date them, but we didn't.

By our junior year we called ourselves the Scoobs, after *Scooby-Doo, Where Are You?*, the much-loved Saturday morning cartoon that followed a group of four young men and women driving around in a cool, multicolored van with their talking Great Dane. They solved mysteries involving ghosts that weren't ghosts but were instead, before each episode ended, unmasked as people, usually carrying out crimes. At first it was just a silly nickname, but soon the jocks and their friends taunted us with it. It had something to do with us listening to New Wave music. Something to do with us driving into Pittsburgh to see *The Gods Must Be Crazy* at an arthouse movie theater. Something to do with us having picnics and going on hikes. Something to do with being smart. There wasn't a big turning point before the moment that changed everything in my head. But high school, a place I loved, quickly became small and stressful. Everything was so *stop being so sensitive*. Everything was *just act normal*. But an energy leaked in from split seams. There was something bigger waiting out there.

I'm at a pep rally my senior year, decked out in my cheerleading uniform, ready to lead the full school in some spirit-raising chants, supporting the exact athletes who heckle and belittle me in the hallways, and suddenly I think: *this is ridiculous*. I squirm in my dictated role. I can feel the expectations that I won't meet trying to corner me into being a *nice girl*. I know I can't be a nice girl. Not on their terms.

At Princeton in 1983, Brooke Shields soon learned it was okay to appear in smart ads created by Richard Avedon, but being actually intelligent wasn't hot for a sex symbol. There just wasn't room for a sexy female nerd in popular culture. No one seemed to believe it was possible that Shields legitimately got into the top-rated school. Comedians had a field day. Johnny Carson, host of *The Tonight Show*, joked about her getting an *A* in anatomy—her own. "At the time, of course, she really was breaking the glass because a sex symbol doesn't go to Princeton," Co-director Jeffrey Alexander notes in the 2023 *Pretty Baby* documentary about Shields's career.

Mary Brice, fellow cheerleader and fellow Scoob, reminded me that, sure, it was technically 1985 when we graduated from high school, but to complicate things even more, our mill town community aligned more with 1979's movie *The Deer Hunter* than 1984's *Sixteen Candles*.

The Deer Hunter is set in Clairton, Pennsylvania, a mill town ten miles south of Pittsburgh. When I google its film locations, a photo of Mingo Junction, Ohio pops up. It's where they shot the bar scenes. For a second I think it's my hometown, Beaver Falls.

Meryl Streep received her first Oscar nomination for her role in the film, which won best picture that year. Streep's character, Linda, is the love interest of Nicky (Christopher Walken), but she also softly sizzles with his best friend Michael (Robert De Niro), both of whom are about to deploy. In the first fifteen minutes of the film, Linda is punched twice by her drunk father as she tries to serve him breakfast in his disheveled second-floor bedroom. After mumbling about flat tires he says, "I fucking mean what I say girl. . . . Fucking bitch, all bitches." Linda wears a pink bridesmaid dress as she spins to the floor from his swinging fist. Her friend Angela is getting married that day to another friend, Steven. Linda stands after the punches, runs a hand across her mouth, smooths her dress, and heads to the church.

The young mill-working men shoot pool in the bar and drink Rolling Rock. A lighted Iron City Beer sign hangs on the wall, and a Pittsburgh Steelers football game plays on the TV. In the first fifteen minutes of the movie the young men are all forward action, bravado, and comradery. They run, slap backs, race cars, boast about hunting deer, and thrive at the center of their close-knit community—the mill at one end of town, the church at the other, a bar in between. They flash money around. These are pre-down-and-out mill-working years.

The young women in the film are objects of affection, lust, violence, and they are servers of food, dance partners, and wives. When interviewed in 1977 by Roger Copeland for *The New York Times*, Streep said about her character, "Linda is essentially a man's view of a woman. She's extremely passive, she's very quiet, she's someone who's constantly vulnerable. . . . Someone who's beaten down a lot by everybody, but who never gets angry about that. . . . I want to break her out of her straitjacket, but of course I can't even let that possibility show. . . . This is a man's movie, it isn't about Linda's problems."

There's no way out for Linda as she and her friends sing "God Bless America" over breakfast beers and shots in the final scene of the movie, but we are perhaps offered a glimpse of another world that exists outside of Linda's constraints when, in the final fifteen minutes of the film, news coverage plays on the bar's TV set.

The seventeen-second clip is of real-life news correspondent Hilary Brown, who covered the fall of Saigon and was one of the last reporters lifted by helicopter from the U.S. Embassy's roof to the USS Hancock. She wears pearl earrings and has tied her hair back with a burgundy scarf that contrasts with her aqua jacket. Brown looks directly into the camera, drawn and serious, as she holds a microphone. "This is the last chapter of American involvement in Vietnam with the largest single movement of people in the history of America," she says. "This is Hilary Brown with ABC News." In 1973 ABC hired Brown as their first woman foreign correspondent.

Senior week, 1985: each day has a different theme. On "Halloween Day," the jocks and their friends come to school wearing "Scoob Busters" T-shirts. The shirts are hand-screened with an image of Scooby-Doo under a red circle with a line through it. The jocks also carry fake plastic guns, modeling themselves on the popular 1984 movie *Ghostbusters*. In the paranormal comedy, three men (Dan Aykroyd, Bill Murray, and Harold Ramis) start a business that eliminates ghosts using a proton pack with a zapping Neutrona Wand. This day, when the Scoob Busters see one of us in the hallway, they shoot us with their fake guns.

They walk throughout the school all day with these guns, to class, to lunch, and then out the doors they push open to leave.

No one gets in trouble as the jocks and their supporters enact their power play in real time, as they affirm the dominance needed for them to remain at the center of our high school community, as they use implied violence to make a statement and maintain the equilibrium.

I double-check with a few Scoobs, now scattered across the country living out their middle age, to make sure this is true. My friend Elmo reminds me that our class president was sent home for coming to "Halloween Day" as a baby with a nipple stretched over a beer can, but everyone agrees that there were no consequences for the Scoob Busters. Later they recycled their T-shirts for their intramural basketball team.

At the MUB, the University of New Hampshire's student union building, students wear vintage army pants and baggy alpaca sweaters and are stationed behind folding tables, passing out pamphlets about anti-apartheid, anti-nuke, Central American and women's solidarity actions. Of course, Young Republicans also scurry about in Izod shirts, topsiders, suits, ties, shoulder pads, and heels. A weird and incongruent mix pulsing through what will be a weird and incongruent decade. It's fall semester, 1985. I don't fit easily into any group. That I had landed in New Hampshire for school, that I wanted to be a creative writer is a baffling fact in and of itself.

It isn't until I move to New Hampshire that my feminism gains context. This happens in the classrooms of the university where I begin to think and talk about inequality, oppression, race, and class in ways that I'd never considered. And it happens in the bakery where I get a job surrounded by strong, opinionated women twenty years my senior. Everyone around me seems leaps ahead in this thinking, and so I work double time to catch up.

Soon I start religiously reading the newly conceived literary journal *The Quarterly*, edited by Gordon Lish. And there they are: living, breathing women writers, writing weird, radical stuff. Amy Hempel, Diane

Williams, and Joy Williams. I soon discover Jayne Anne Phillips's *Black Tickets* and Susan Minot's *Lust*. Hello. There, at last, are the women writers I've been looking for, writing about lonely, lusty women searching for a place to call home. Add Raymond Carver to the reading mix, along with some working-class tension and layered silences, and I find my voice.

Quarterly West publishes my first short story in 1990. "It's Bob, Let's Say, or John" has a first-person narrator who slips in and out of second person and who insists she always keeps her lovers' names straight. She meets a recent lover, Bob, on the street, who forgets her name.

"You could walk away—just keep going, keep feeling good, but that's not how you do things," I write. "So, you do the thing you know best. You smile; shrug. Kind of. You tell him it's okay; he wasn't that good in bed anyway." The narrator in my story understands it isn't cool to care but also questions why, acknowledging the expectation of how a liberated woman should act and the why of the tension behind it all. "The fact of the matter is, you remember his name, but he doesn't remember yours," I write at the story's end. "And you know there is something wrong with that. But you can't figure out what it is."

"In the early 1990s, young [white] middle-class women took to the streets to protest the erosion of abortion and reproductive rights, gathered in coffee shops and dorm rooms to discuss their personal experiences with sexism and violence, and assembled in punk rock nightclubs and hijacked typically masculine spaces in order to stage their own creative and political actions," writes Elizabeth Ann Bly in her dissertation "Generation X and the Invention of a Third Feminist Wave."

By the '90s many of us had dropped out and chosen to become free-spirited nerds. Walked away from Love's Baby Soft's "Innocence is Sexy" campaign and into essential oils and zines, road trips and angry bands. We stepped out of the mainstream and into a complicated third wave.

I eventually hit the road a year after graduating from college. I leave New England in 1991 for the Bay Area in a slow, staggered migration across the United States with various writer and musician friends. I discover Mary Gaitskill and M. F. K. Fisher, Liz Phair, the Breeders, and the Throwing Muses. I meet old-school hippies and newly minted Riot Grrrls. The AIDS crisis and homelessness and drug addiction are all there in the city in front of me. The world and its complexities expand in my head. I work and write. I bake and read. There's a glorious fluidity that's laid bare in San Francisco. The idea of gender becomes multifaceted as it slides around on the dance floor. I play pool in the lesbian bars. I meet sad, elderly queens in cocktail bars. I walk and walk and walk across the city, across the Golden Gate Bridge. I save money to take road trips so I can come back and work to save money for road trips. I suck it in and then my brain is ready for grad school. Ready to put it all back together again in a classroom, which ends up being located in Nebraska, of all places.

Perhaps I immediately took to film theory in my mid-1990s grad school classes because I was used to the idea of being male-gazed-upon so overtly in my teen years. "There are circumstances in which looking itself is a source of pleasure, just as, in the reverse formation, there is pleasure in being looked at," writes Laura Mulvey in her seminal 1975 essay "Visual Pleasure and Narrative Cinema." Yes, I think. I know this second pleasure. Throughout my teenhood I fully understood it was my job to be seen, not for who I was, but for what I represented. I was the sleeping Victorian woman painted beside the stream with long, flowing hair. My job was to sleep beautifully. No one directly taught me I was an object. I just came to know it like I came to know breathing. My job was to be looked upon. In some ways, in many ways, it felt exceptional. Just by existing I held a kind of power. It didn't seem complicated, and then it really did.

"Feminism . . . equates the male gaze with patriarchy. Patriarchy defines a social system . . . women depend not only for status and privilege, but for their very identity, upon men," writes Mary Devereaux in "Oppressive Texts, Resisting Readers and the Gendered Spectator: The New Aesthetics" in the fall 1990 issue of *The Journal of Aesthetics and Art Criticism*. Devereaux notes that it's the first piece of feminist theory ever published by the journal.

"As [Simone] de Beauvoir explains," Devereaux continues, "women, unlike men, do not learn to describe the world from their own point of view. As the 'other,' woman learns to submerge or renounce her subjectivity. She finds her identity in the subjectivity of the men to whom she is attached (father, husband, lover). In the eyes of men, she finds her identity as the object of men's desire." Yes, I say, as I read this passage, curled into an armchair in the living room of my Lincoln, Nebraska, apartment in 1994. Coffee at my elbow, my cat Nicki snoozing on her back in the middle of the floor, *Exile from Guyville* playing from a boombox wedged into a corner just outside my kitchen, reminding me that men fuck and run.

In class I learn that the entirety of society is shaped to oppress women without our knowing it, that we all filter the entire world through the male gaze. Of course. I already know this, but learning the language academia wants us to use to talk about it as we discuss films and texts breaks open a new level of knowing and a new degree of frustration with society. It's exhilarating and challenging material. Thinking about how the cinema works like a set of eyes helps me see the world more clearly as I sit in the classroom, a bug under a microscope. My slow-simmering knowledge rumbling like water in a kettle.

At night my friend Liz Champlin and I play pool against men who try to cheat us at eight ball in the bars of Lincoln. We bear witness to our building rage in real time out in the untheoretical world. Pool table center stage, a shaded beer sign shining down, our spotlight. Music thumps. Balls clack. Men lean forward to see what they can see down our shirts.

At this time people ask, *Why are you so angry?* and at the time I can only think, *Why isn't everyone?* I embed as much feminist, film, and critical theory as I can stand into my brain and try to outmaneuver my classmates by using linguistic gymnastics in my seminar classes.

"As I saw mills closing, families suffering, and men angry I knew that I NEVER wanted to be dependent on someone else . . . and a 'woman's' job wasn't gonna cut it," Mary Brice writes to me in an email. Petite and wiry, Mary is buff, a runner, an ultimate frisbee player, and a mother of three. She distinctly remembers thinking she needed a "man's job" around seventh or eighth grade.

While I wrote poems and stories, she walked work sites. She's now a civil engineering consultant in Raleigh, North Carolina.

But she was also a cheerleader with me in ninth through twelfth grade. We were in the Scrabble Club and roller-skated at Homewood Roller Rink nearly every weekend in middle school. "All of my working life I've interacted with loads of men, which all women in engineering are accustomed to," she continues, "but I especially enjoy my interactions with the blue-collar guys: construction crews, maintenance workers, equipment operators. They are largely a tattooed, hairy, Harley-riding bunch with whom I have NO qualms interacting. Speaking that language has been an asset."

In September 2018 Professor Christine Blasey Ford steps up to a table to testify about Brett Kavanaugh, a Supreme Court nominee, to the Senate Judiciary Committee. Ford is fifty-two years old. She has a practical but stylish shoulder-length haircut, fashionable but nerdy eyeglasses, and wears a well-tailored dark blue suit. She looks and sounds like what she is: a reliable Gen-X narrator and hardworking professor. Ford claims Kavanaugh attempted to rape her at a high school party in 1982 when she was fifteen years old and Kavanaugh seventeen. "Brett groped me and tried to take off my clothes," she tells the committee. "He had a hard time because he was so drunk and because I was wearing a one-piece bathing suit under my clothes. I believed he was going to rape me. I tried to yell for help. When I did, Brett put his hand over my mouth to stop me from screaming. This was what terrified me the most and has had the most lasting impact on my life."

In a 1983 Georgetown Prep yearbook entry, which Kavanaugh wrote, he lists himself as a "Renate Alumnius," [sic] a reference to Renate Schroeder, a student attending a nearby all-girls school. Many young men at the school create entries referencing her. There's a group photograph of football players, including Kavanaugh, captioned "Renate Alumni." The assumption is these are true or made-up boastful sexual conquests of Schroeder, who later withdrew her signature from a letter supporting Kavanaugh. Other terms included in Kavanaugh's entry include "Devil's Triangle" and "Boof," which have their own history of describing sexual acts achieved or wished for. A threesome with two men and anal sex respectively. The yearbook also includes many references to drinking, which is a topic that spills over into the committee meeting itself. The country soon understands that Brett Kavanaugh likes beer.

Kavanaugh, sculpted hair, pasty skin, black suit with a white shirt and royal blue necktie, adamantly denies the claims as he sits before the committee. "I look back at high school and cringe for some things," he says. "For one thing, our yearbook was a disaster. I think some editors and students wanted the yearbook to be some combination of *Animal House, Caddyshack*, and *Fast Times at Ridgemont High*, which were all recent movies at that time."

The three films Kavanaugh cites during his Senate Committee testimony are considered late-'70s and early '80s teen classics, instantly part of the teen lexicon and culture of the time, instantly hilarious, all designated as comedy/romance in the IMDb database. In retrospect they really aren't that funny. Or romantic. They are awash in the terms, viewpoints, and sexual dominance of men.

In *Animal House* (1978), for example, a woman passes out drunk after she's been making out with Pinto, a new pledge. By this time she's topless, and Pinto contemplates sexually assaulting her, with an angel and a devil playing out options on his shoulders. "Fuck her brains out," the devil says. "Squeeze her buns. You know she wants it."

The 2023 Oscar ceremony streams on my friend Hattie Fletcher's computer in an Airbnb apartment she's rented near the Seattle Convention Center. We're attending the annual Association of Writers & Writing Programs (AWP) conference, and as it winds up, we wind down with a baguette, cheese, wine, and two exquisite macarons that we stood in line like tourists to buy at Pike Place Market. We've put on soft pants and excused ourselves from interacting with the outside world until we catch our flight back to Pittsburgh the next morning.

"But is feminism about sex?" Hattie asks, reaching for her wine glass, tucking her legs up on the couch.

"Yes," I say. Then some time passes, and I say, "Isn't it?"

In between critiquing actors' gown choices and congratulating ourselves on our cheese selections, we're in-real-life continuing a conversation that started in a group WhatsApp thread the week before, trying to answer the unexpectedly difficult question: *What is feminism?*

At the ceremony unfolding in front of us on Hattie's tiny screen, fellow Gen Xer Sarah Polley wins the Oscar for best adapted screenplay for *Women Talking*, an adaptation of the novel by Miriam Toews. Based on a true story from 2005, the movie follows a group of Mennonite women who secretly meet in a barn to discuss whether to stay and stay quiet, stay and fight, or leave after being routinely drugged and raped by men from their community.

Polley takes the stage wearing a tux instead of a gown. She clutches the statue with two hands. "First of all," she says, "I want to thank the academy for not being mortally offended by 'women' and 'talking' being so close together like that."

Our Scrappy Motherfuckers WhatsApp chat, a group of six women writers and editors, started in March 2020 after a random night of raucous cocktails in Pittsburgh in lieu of attending an AWP conference. We met up right before COVID-19 lockdown at a hotel bar that seemed out of a movie set, high up on the hotel's tenth floor with good cocktails, sparkly blue lights, and a lot of plate glass windows.

At first the feed focused on forwarding COVID-19 facts and handy information and, if I'm being honest, lipstick recommendations, but now it's like we're all next-door neighbor philosophers wandering out into our yards at all times of the day and night with a cup of coffee or a short pour of whiskey, talking over a fence about . . . everything. When we do something that moves our world or the bigger world forward we hashtag it with #action. Laundry done? #action. Disrupted a city council meeting to fight for the removal of the open-air police firing range in a residential neighborhood? #action. Editor subverted who was undermining the publication? #action. It's a small daily record of forward movement. Some posts would make great cross-stitch pillows, we point out. "MEN DO THIS SHIT" is one example. But we never actually do the stitching. Maybe someday one of us will take on this task and then it, too, will be an #action. For now we get ourselves and each other through everything from making dinner to negotiating a book contract to defining feminism to picking up a kid from play practice.

Recently Joy posted a bio for the Pistol Annies, a singer-songwriting trio that "can sound both rootsy and progressive at the same time, taking on the conventions of honky-tonk and Southern rock with a feminist's sense of humor and some bracing real talk," and added, "I thought of you, @Sherrie."

The bio continues: "A woman in an Annies' ballad might daydream . . . about setting her own house on fire ('Housewife's Prayer') while an ode to sticking with it for the long haul ('Unhappily Married') . . . manages to make it sound cheerful."

"This is my feminism. What is it called?" I write. "Who Gives a Fuck Feminism? Let's Kick Some Ass Feminism? Fuck Off Feminism? Jesus Christ Get Your Shit Together Feminism?"

Joy responds, "Is this one of your essay's paragraphs?"

"I really need to swear more in the essay," I reply, which is met with a thumbs-up, salt shaker, and laughing face emoji as we head into a discussion of the recent "You're Wrong About" podcast addressing *The New York Times'* messed up reporting on trans issues.

During the Judiciary Committee meeting, Senator Patrick Leahy asks Christine Blasey Ford to relay what memory still strongly remained with her all these years after the attack. "Indelible in the hippocampus is the laughter," she says, "the uproarious laughter between the two and their having fun at my expense."

In addition to all the sports and cheerleading, I happen to be co-editor of the Blackhawk High School yearbook. One day our photographer submits a shot of the Scoob Busters proudly posing with their fake guns and tees against a set of lockers in our school's hallway with their Levi's jeans, mirrored sunglasses, Timberland boots, and hard hats, with their charming smiles and fit bodies. I print it in the book in full color. Because even then, I know at some point in the future, people will say it never happened.

Intent. Did Brett Kavanaugh have sexual conquests or just brag about them in his high school yearbook? Did the Scoob Busters want to shoot us, or was it just a joke? As Ford points out, that laughter lodges in our hippocampi. One group ends up laughing, and that laughter gives them the power to do whatever the hell they want, and it prevents those of us on the receiving end from keeping our brains clear of the impact, big and small. It sometimes makes us on that end reconsider how we're going to live our lives.

I recently started cleaning out my eighty-seven-year-old parents' attic. Their house, my childhood home, is filled with a lot of stuff, some of it mine. In the past few weeks I've traveled the nostalgic roller-coaster from childhood to adolescence to college to grad school to my wedding napkins.

Last week I found my Barbies wedged in the back of a dark and gritty crawlspace. I dragged out their airplane, bike, pool, and Dream House. Four plastic Barbie cases covered in colorful '70s designs with silver buckles along the side housed seven Barbies and a Ken doll. So many Barbies staring vacantly out into 2023 saying, What the fuck is going on?

With their pointy feet and their tiny waists, their barely bending arms and legs and awkwardly braided hair, the last time they saw the light of day it was the swinging '70s. Their extra sets of mod outfits jammed into a separate kid's suitcase—and shoes, Barbie shoes everywhere—they were ready for a spin at the disco or a legal abortion in all fifty states. They could set out to get a good union job at the mill, but no, they couldn't run over a mile in competition.

Until recently I probably wouldn't have admitted until pretty far into a happy hour to playing with Barbie dolls. I rarely tell anyone I was a cheerleader. I thought these activities revealed a flaw in my girl-hood upbringing, a softness, a buying into. But I had so many Barbies.

Playing Barbies meant playing stories, working out character and plot. Sure, these plastic women couldn't stand up on their own, but when haven't obstacles and mixed messages been unfolding all around me?

The odds have always been against Barbie. She falls down. Not a new story, but it's part of a story I can tell, of learning to stand to run to leave to find home to leave again and again, only to return to where I started, changed.

SOURCE ACKNOWLEDGMENTS

The author would like to thank the journals and magazines that originally published many of these essays, some in different forms.

Belt Magazine: "Faith in Movement"

The Best American Poetry blog: "Faith in Movement" (as "Drinks with Poets: Peter Oresick")

Fried Walleye and Cherry Pie: Midwestern Writers on Food (University of Nebraska Press): "Calling Me Out" (as "The Tam-O-Shanter, Lincoln, Nebraska")

Heated: "Rebel Rebel"

New England Review: "All in the Family: Waldo and His Ghosts"

Pittsburgh Quarterly: "Finding Home" (as "The Egg Route")

Ploughshares: "Caretaker, Murderer, Undertaker"; "The Worst Possible Offense"

Western Pennsylvania History magazine: "Talk Right"

Borderline Citizen: Dispatches from the Outskirts of Nationhood
by Robin Hemley

The Distance Between: A Memoir
by Timothy J. Hillegonds

Opa Nobody
by Sonya Huber

Pain Woman Takes Your Keys, and Other Essays from a Nervous System
by Sonya Huber

Hannah and the Mountain: Notes toward a Wilderness Fatherhood
by Jonathan Johnson

Under My Bed and Other Essays
by Jody Keisner

Local Wonders: Seasons in the Bohemian Alps
by Ted Kooser

A Certain Loneliness: A Memoir
by Sandra Gail Lambert

Bigger than Life: A Murder, a Memoir
by Dinah Lenney

What Becomes You
by Aaron Raz Link and Hilda Raz

Queen of the Fall: A Memoir of Girls and Goddesses
by Sonja Livingston

The Virgin of Prince Street: Expeditions into Devotion
by Sonja Livingston

Anything Will Be Easy after This: A Western Identity Crisis
by Bethany Maile

Such a Life
by Lee Martin

Turning Bones
by Lee Martin

In Rooms of Memory: Essays
by Hilary Masters

Island in the City: A Memoir
by Micah McCrary

Between Panic and Desire
by Dinty W. Moore

To Hell with It: Of Sin and Sex, Chicken Wings, and Dante's Entirely Ridiculous, Needlessly Guilt-Inducing Inferno
by Dinty W. Moore

Let Me Count the Ways: A Memoir
by Tomás Q. Morín

Shadow Migration: Mapping a Life
by Suzanne Ohlmann

Meander Belt: Family, Loss, and Coming of Age in the Working-Class South
by M. Randal O'Wain

Sleep in Me
by Jon Pineda

The Solace of Stones: Finding a Way through Wilderness
by Julie Riddle

To order or obtain more information on these or other University of Nebraska Press titles, visit nebraskapress.unl.edu.

www.ingramcontent.com/pod-product-compliance
Lightning Source LLC
Chambersburg PA
CBHW021402090426
42742CB00009B/973